SOLD INTO EGYPT

Madeleine L'Engle
SOLD INTO EGYPT

Joseph's Journey into Human Being

Harold Shaw Publishers
Wheaton, Illinois

The Wheaton Literary Series

Copyright © Crosswicks, 1989

ISBN 0-87788-766-7

Cover photo © 1989 by Luci Shaw

Library of Congress Cataloging-in-Publication Data

L'Engle, Madeleine.
    Sold into Egypt / Madeleine L'Engle.
      p.   cm. — (Wheaton literary series)
    ISBN 0-87788-766-7
    1. Joseph (Son of Jacob)   2. Bible stories, English—O.T.
Genesis. 3. Patriarchs (Bible) I. Title. II. Series.
BS580.J6L46   1989
222'.1109505—dc20
                                            89-32030
                                            CIP

98 97 96 95 94 93 92 91 90 89

10 9   8 7 6 5 4 3 2

for
Margaret and Charles
Esther and Carol

CONTENTS

The story of Joseph is the journey of a spoiled and selfish young man finally becoming, through betrayal, anger, abandonment, unfairness, and pain, a full and complex human being. I have much to learn from his story. So do we all.

Madeleine L'Engle

Reuben

thou art my firstborn, my might, and the beginning (first fruits) of my strength, the excellency of dignity, and the excellency of power:

Unstable as water, thou shalt not excel; because thou wentest up to thy father's bed; then defiledst thou it: he went up to my couch.

Genesis 49:3-4

Reuben
1

HE WAS A SPOILED BRAT, Joseph, the eleventh brother. Indulged, self-indulgent, selfish. He clung to his father and the women. Whined. Got his own way. If one of the wives said no, another would surely say yes. When he was crossed he wailed that he had no mother. His older brothers took off in the other direction whenever he came around.

In his adolescence he became arrogant. He knew that he was the favoured one of the twelve brothers, but he was not yet old enough to know that a father does a son no favour in singling him out, giving him a beautiful coat, lavishing him with love.

He dreamed big dreams, and he was not wise enough to keep them to himself.

Pouring fuel on the fire of his brothers' resentment one day, he said, "Listen to this dream I have dreamed! We were binding sheaves in the field, and my sheaf rose and stood upright. And all your sheaves stood round about, and bowed down to my sheaf."

Not surprisingly, his brothers were angry. "Will you reign over us indeed? Will you have dominion over us?" And they hated him all the more because of his dreams and his bragging.

Joseph could not keep his dreams quietly in his heart, but went on boasting. "Listen. I have dreamed another dream! In this dream the sun and the moon and the eleven stars bowed to me."

This time even his father Jacob scolded him, saying, "What is this dream that you have dreamed? Shall your mother and your brothers indeed come to bow down before you?"

Which mother was Jacob referring to? Rachel was dead—Rachel who had borne Joseph, and then died, giving birth to little Benjamin. Was Jacob thinking of Leah, Rachel's elder sister, who had given him six sons and a daughter? Or Bilhah or Zilpah, the maids, who had each given him two sons? Or was he, deep in his heart, still thinking of Rachel, the one he most loved? Could it be, that after all these years, more than ten, Jacob still did not, deep in his heart, believe in Rachel's death?

There is something in all of us that shares this disbelief, especially after we have lost those dearest to us. I still want to turn to my mother, saying, "Mother, you're the only one who knows about this—" It is a reflex that will never completely vanish. The mortal fact of my husband Hugh's death is still, sometimes, a matter for total disbelief.

Many African tribes do not believe in the deaths of their members, but hold that they are still available, can be talked to, conferred with, asked for advice. Across the world and across time in the Episcopal Church (and in other liturgical churches) we celebrate All Saints' Day and talk about that great cloud of witnesses with which we are surrounded—all those, known and unknown, who have gone before us. We talk of the communion of saints, and by saints we mean not only those especially endowed with holiness, but the saints as all of God's people. This communion is the gift to us of the Resurrection. So, although the death of this mortal body is undeniable, in a very deep way we do not believe in death. I believe that it was Rachel in Jacob's heart when he referred to "your mother." Joseph's mother in fact. Jacob's beloved always.

Joseph's brothers were poisoned by envy. But his father observed and thought about what Joseph had told about his dreams. Perhaps the old man was secretly proud that his favoured son was going to be a great man. He was rich, old Jacob, having settled in the land of Canaan, but keeping himself apart from the natives who worshipped alien gods. These natives were, in fact, distant cousins, being descended from Noah's son, Ham. But they worshipped the storm god Baal, giver of rain, which was desperately needed in this desert land; and they worshipped Mot, a god who could strike those he disliked with sterility and death. Goddesses were part of the Canaanite pantheon, too, fertility goddesses who ruled over the crops and animals.

Jacob held to the one god he had chosen, the God of his father, Isaac, and his grandfather, Abraham. And he prospered; his flocks increased in number so much that his sons had to take the beasts further and further afield to find pasture.

Joseph, the braggart, like the baby brother, Benjamin, was not given his full share of the work, and this, too, was resented. Joseph was fourteen, more than old enough to pull his own weight. In those days so many thousands of years ago, a lad was a man at fourteen, and most girls were married, and had borne children.

Being the favoured one is lonely. Benjamin, the baby, was pampered in a different way, adored by Dinah, the one sister, worshipped by the two concubines. He was happy, easily pleased, demanded little. He did not remember his mother and accepted, without question, the mothering of the other women. He was not a question-asker.

But Joseph was inquisitive, wanting to know every-thing.

"Why does the moon get bigger and then smaller and then bigger?" He was not satisfied when Bilhah, who had been Rachel's maid, told him that the goddess ruled the moon. "What is the goddess like? Is she beautiful? Why don't we have a goddess? Does a goddess look like my mother?"

Bilhah put her finger to her lips. "Hush."

"Why?"

"Your father doesn't approve of goddesses."

He turned to Zilpah, Leah's maid. "Why is the sun so hot that it withers the crops? Why did El put the stars in the sky since they're not bright enough to see by? Why?"

When he was given answers, they were simple, be-cause the world then was a smaller and simpler world than ours. The sun and the moon and the stars were put in the sky by the Creator for the benefit of human beings. Crops, calving, lambing, all were determined by the rhythm of the heavenly bodies which in turn determined the essential rain, and the cycles of the females of all species. The cosmology of creation was accepted, rather than understood. It was a knowledge which had been passed down from Abraham to Isaac, from Isaac to Jacob, and which Jacob was now passing on to his twelve sons.

Twelve sons. Four mothers. Polygamy was customary. There were more women than men. The planet was sparsely populated and sons were important. *"As arrows are in the hand of a mighty man, so are the children of the youth. Happy the man that hath his quiver full of them; they shall not be ashamed, but they shall speak with the enemies in the gate."* Thus spoke the psalmist centuries later.

For a man to have a quiver full of sons, he needed more than one wife and, in addition, concubines. As far as we know, it was not the custom for a woman to have more than one husband. Because men were killed in skirmishes with other tribes, or by wild animals when they were out hunting, there were extra women, and surely it seemed the kindest thing to take these otherwise superfluous women into the family circle as wives. Customs tend to reflect the realities of a time and culture. We, of the late twentieth century, have tended to impose our own mores on others, without trying to find out why certain customs have arisen. Because we have failed to listen to each other's stories, we are becoming a fragmented human race.

I try to listen to the story of Joseph and his brothers, and of his father, Jacob, because it is a story of human beings becoming more human through their adventures and misadventures. The story of Joseph is the journey of a spoiled and selfish young man finally becoming, through betrayal, anger, abandonment, unfairness, and pain, a full and complex human being. I have much to learn from his story.

Jacob and his sons lived in a masculine world, with a masculine God, surrounded by alien deities, many of them feminine, who directed the planting of the crops. It was a polytheistic world full of rivalry, each tribe convinced of the superiority of its own particular deity. The

One God of the Hebrew, the God who is One, the God who is All, was still remote. A pantheon of gods was accepted by our forbears, as the psalmist makes quite clear: *"Whose god is like unto our god?"* Or, *"Among the gods there is none like unto thee, O Lord; there is not one that can do what you do."* It was normal to assume that one's own particular god was more potent than other peoples' gods.

And yet for Joseph and his family there was also the paradoxical and contradictory belief that God, the Creator, had made everything, the earth with its seas and land masses and all the various species of fish and birds and animals and finally, as the culmination, the triumph of creation, man—male and female. *Homo sapiens*, the creature who knows. We know that we know and consequently we ask unanswerable questions.

Joseph's questions were simpler than ours, but still questions.

When Joseph's mother, Rachel, left the home of her father, Laban, the home where she had grown up, where she had married Jacob, where she had finally given birth to Joseph, she took with her—stole—her father's household gods, her teraphim, the little clay creatures who might make the rain fall, the sun burn less harshly, the journey safe. But they had not kept Rachel from death, those little teraphim. They were idols, man-made things. What kind of power did they have? Why did Rachel treasure them enough to steal them from her father? To lie, in order to keep them? Why?

And where were her teraphim now that she was dead and the rest of the family was settled in Canaan? Had Jacob given them back to his father-in-law, Laban? Joseph—the questioner, the dreamer—had overheard the concubines talking about the lost teraphim and, secretly, had searched for them, but found no trace of the little figures.

The other brothers did not have the time or inclination for questions, or even to remember their dreams. Life was rugged. They had to tend the animals, take them to pasture, make sure the women brought enough water from the well for human and animal needs, keep the cook fires going, peg down the nomad tents in case of sudden wind. The more successful Jacob, the patriarch, became, the more work there was for his sons.

It was good for Jacob to keep busy. It helped to assuage his unremitting grief over the death of Rachel, the one woman he truly loved. The other women? Oh, they gave him sons, and sons were valuable, but it was Rachel who was loved, Rachel who died giving birth to Benjamin, Rachel for whom he grieved.

How hard it must have been for Leah, his first wife. The Book of Genesis suggests that Leah was cross-eyed. Certainly she was not beautiful, like Rachel. But she bore him six sons, and his undying grief for her sister may well have seemed to her yet another rejection.

But we do not choose who we love, and Jacob loved Rachel.

In these late years of the twentieth century it seems to be more usual for a woman to outlive her husband than vice versa. In the early Genesis days the patriarchs buried their wives, dead in childbirth, or worn out from childbearing. The patriarchs grieved, went on living, sometimes remarrying and having children in their old age like Abraham. Old age was treasured, revered, not hidden away because then, as now, it was a reminder that we all grow old and die. In Deuteronomy 34:7 we read, *And Moses was an hundred and twenty years old when he died:*

his eye was not dim, nor his natural force abated. What a triumph that Moses, dying at a venerable age, still had "his juices"!

Not long after I started working on this book my husband became ill, and I lived with the story of Joseph during his dying and his death. I grieve for my husband, and as time goes by the grief does not lessen. Rather, as the shock wears off, it deepens, and through my own grief I have at least a flicker of understanding of Jacob's continuing grief for Rachel. Hugh and I were married for forty years. How long were Jacob and Rachel married? Not quite that long, but long enough. Dinah, the one daughter, Leah's last child, born before Joseph and Benjamin were born to Rachel, was old enough to be married before Benjamin was born.

And love cannot be timed, judged chronologically. Love transcends time. And the love of one human being for another transcends animal sex (which is sheerly for the purpose of procreation). The human being, it would seem, is the only being whose love-making is not limited to the reproduction of the species, who makes love for the sheer joy of loving. It is the depth and width of love that makes us human.

Human. How do we become human? What does it mean to be human? We human creatures seem to become less and less human as this sorry century staggers to a close. We have been made dependent on Social Security numbers, on plastic credit cards; we are overwhelmed by paper forms in duplicate and triplicate and quadruplicate. The amount of legal/financial paperwork following Hugh's death was staggering, not to mention the personal correspondence.

Jacob, after Rachel's death, had no such problems with banks, Social Security, insurance. I've had to produce papers to prove that I was born ("Since I'm standing here, talking to you, it seems quite evident that I was born." Still I was told, "You must produce your birth certificate."), or that I was married; sign affidavits that I was still married to Hugh at the time of his death, that we were not divorced or living separately. Our joint bank account was frozen, and I was made very aware that this is still a male-dominated and male-chauvinist society, less paternalistic, perhaps, than in Jacob's day, but equally male-oriented. Hugh and I had had that account for over twenty-five years, and yet I had to prove that I, Madeleine, the *ux*, the wife, in this case, was capable of having a bank account. (Occasionally, even today, in financial or legal documents, the wife is still referred to with the Latin *ux*, for *uxor*—woman.) Fortunately I also had my own personal bank account in another bank, or I would have been hard-pressed to pay my bills during the quarter of a year it took me to get that bank account activated. One reason I had always had my own bank account was that a friend, after her husband's sudden death, had to live on the charity of friends until the bank where she had a joint account deemed that she had a right to have her own account there.

Someone said that all this paperwork gives the bereaved something to do. But I don't think that's it at all. The paperwork protects everybody who encounters the bereaved person from her—or his—grief. If there is a lot of paperwork to be done we can forget that we, too, may lose the one dearest to us. We can put out of our minds the fact that we, too, one day will die. The impersonality of paperwork emphasizes our inhumanity, whereas grief is one of the most human of all emotions.

Rachel died, and Jacob grieved. It wouldn't surprise me if he had gone out into the desert and howled his anguish, away from the tents and the campfires, alone, on the strange journey to Canaan. The ancient people of Genesis were human. Imperfect, like us; but human.

Why are we so afraid to be human, depending on legalism and moralism and dogmatism instead? Jesus came to us as a truly human being, to show us how to be human, and we were so afraid of this humanness that we crucified it, thinking it could be killed. And today we are still afraid to be human, struggling instead with a perfectionism which is crippling, or which in some cases can lead to a complete moral breakdown. We are not perfect. Only God is perfect. And God does not ask us to be perfect; God asks us to be human. This means to know at all times that we are God's children, never to lose our connection with our Creator. Jesus was sinless not because he didn't do wrong things: he broke the law, picking corn, for instance, on the Sabbath. He was sinless because he was never for a moment separated from the Source.

We are called to be God's holy and human people. What has happened? This falling away from our calling is nothing new. Jeremiah called the people of his day—the people of God—a horror and a hissing and an everlasting reproach. Jeremiah, once he had accepted his calling, did not hesitate to say what needed to be said, and nobody likes being called a horror and a hissing and an everlasting reproach.

What would that bank official, with his cigar, and his assumption that because I was a woman I wasn't capable of having my own bank account, what would he have done if I had called him a horror and a hissing and an everlasting reproach? It would certainly have slowed things down even further, so I held my peace.

Those who are a horror and a hissing and an everlasting reproach have failed to be human. When we are totally centred on legalism, or when we are totally centred on self (as the adolescent Joseph was totally centred on himself and his vainglory), we are unable to be human. When we, like Joseph, are centred on our own power we have alienated ourselves not only from our brethren (or sistren or friends or bank clients or patients) but from God, and from the possibility of being truly human.

Odd contradiction here: this has been called the "me" generation; the emphasis on self-gratification is epidemic. Yet we are also a generation alienated by our legalism, I.D. cards, numbering, all the impersonalism that dehumanizes us. Perhaps the two go together: over-emphasis on self results in loss of self.

Joseph, in his pride, alienated himself (it is interesting that psychiatrists used to be called alienists). But Joseph's alienation was a result of his father's favouritism, which turned a potentially nice child into a nasty brat. If Jacob had understood himself better he might have been a more understanding parent. But Jacob was a complicated man, unable to say "I'm sorry" for any of his trickery and cheating, and therefore unable to accept forgiveness. He was never able to acknowledge that his behavior towards his brother Esau was selfish and unscrupulous, and so he was not able to accept himself.

Of course the assumption throughout the centuries (and, it would seem, especially today) has been that unscrupulosity is fine as long as you don't get caught. It's all right to cheat on an exam as long as nobody sees you doing it. It's all right to fudge on income tax as long as you can get away with it. Shady business deals are simply the nature of the world.

Jacob's cheating of Esau was in keeping with this philosophy of instant gratification at any cost—especially if the cost was to someone else. Some people seem to manage to cheat and lie and wheel-and-deal with no pangs of conscience—at least no conscious ones. But I suspect there is an inward gnawing, as there was with Jacob.

It is an amazing thing that Jacob wrestled with an angel and yet seldom wrestled with himself. And he bequeathed his complexity to his family as, indeed, in one way or another, do we all. The story of Jacob and his twelve sons and one daughter is a family story, and all interesting families are complicated, as I know from experience.

The psalmist sings, in Coverdale's translation, *"Behold, how good and joyful a thing it is, for brethren to dwell together in unity."* It is a cry of wistfulness rather than of triumph, because throughout Scripture, as through life, brothers seldom dwell together in perfect unity. Many of the psalms are attributed to David, and certainly David's children were not able to dwell together in unity. There was infidelity and lust. There was incest. There was Absalom turning against his father and battling him for the kingdom. There was quarreling and bickering and jostling for power.

And so, it seems, it has always been with the human race, beginning with the family of Adam and Eve.

The first lines of Tolstoi's *Anna Karenina* are, "Happy families are all alike. Every unhappy family is unhappy in its own way."

What is a happy family—a perfectly happy family? I'm not sure. I suspect it doesn't exist, the family that lives in constant concord, with no lost tempers, no raised

voices, where everybody smiles and is unfailingly courteous. No. Wait. As a matter of fact I have encountered
one family where everybody smiled and was unfailingly
courteous, and underneath the surface perfection I sensed
barely banked rage and terrible unhappiness.

Joseph and his brothers did not dwell together in
unity. And yet as the story unfolds we see that they *were*
family, in the deepest sense of the word. Happiness is not
a criterion for the truest kind of family loving, any more
than instant gratification is a criterion for joy. There seems
to be an illusion in some of Christendom today that Christians are always happy. No matter what tragedies happen, Christians are supposed to be happy if they truly
have faith. It's only an illusion and can cause enormous
trouble. Jesus was not always happy. He was, indeed, the
suffering servant Isaiah talks about. Happiness, blind, un-
questioning happiness, is not the sign of the Christian.
Even the Holy Family was not, in the superficial sense of
the word, happy. Simeon warned Mary that a sword of
anguish would penetrate her own heart. And, indeed, it
did.

Usually in Scripture when it is predicted that a sword
is going to pierce the heart, it is the heart of the enemy, the
marauder, the violent man, as in Psalm 37: *"The ungodly
have drawn out the sword, and have bent their bow, to cast
down the poor and needy, and to slay such as be upright in their
ways. Their sword shall go through their own heart, and their
bow shall be broken."*

But Simeon makes this prediction to Mary, the mother
of Jesus. *When Mary's days of purification according to the
laws of Moses were accomplished, they brought [the baby] to
Jerusalem to present him to the Lord. And there was in the
temple an old man who had been told by the Holy Spirit that he*

would not die before he had seen the Messiah. He recognized the baby as the Lord's Christ, and took him up in his arms, saying, "Now, Lord, let your servant depart in peace." These words, the "Nunc dimittis" from Luke, are sung or said daily in the evening office in the Episcopal Church. During the long days of my husband's dying they came to have new and poignant meaning for me.

After these familiar words Simeon goes on to say to Mary, *"A sword is going to pierce through your own soul."*

Surely this happened more than once. What anguish Mary felt when Jesus was a boy of twelve and disappeared, and his parents searched for him frantically. I remember my own sense of panic when my little boy vanished in a crowded department store, and the surge of relief when I found him. I expect most mothers have gone through a similar experience.

A sword must have pierced Mary's heart again when she sought Jesus and he said, *"Who is my Mother?"* seemingly disowning her. She watched him moving further and further away from his family as his earthly ministry proceeded. And she watched him die, like a common criminal, on a cross, between two thieves.

And yet Jesus' family was a holy family. As all families are called on to be holy; with all our differences, opinionatedness, selfishness, we are redeemed by a love which is deeper than all our brokenness, a love given to us when the Maker of the Universe came to Mary's womb, to show incredible love for us all by becoming one of us. And so the holiness of all families was affirmed.

By the time that Jesus was born in Nazareth it had become the norm in his part of the world for a family to consist of one husband and one wife. But at the time of the story of Joseph and his brothers this was not so. Family and sexual mores had a pattern different from ours. It was a permissible (though not laudable) part of the moral code for both Abraham and Isaac to pass their wives off as their sisters to King Abimelech and his son, because the code permitted the Philistines to sleep with a man's sister, but not his wife. Odd indeed that seems to us. But it was a different world, the world of the patriarchs, indeed a patriarchal world, and we will not even begin to understand it if we try to apply twentieth-century standards to it.

Jacob's family, his two wives, their maids, and twelve sons and one daughter, was the family which began the twelve tribes of Israel. And how different Jacob's children must have been, with four different mothers.

Leah	Bilhah	Zilpah	Rachel
Reuben			
Simeon			
Levi			
Judah			
	Dan		
	Naphtali		
		Gad	
		Asher	
Issachar			
Zebulun			
Dinah			
			Joseph
			Benjamin

Jacob had been tricked into marrying Leah before he married his beloved Rachel, and Leah bore him Reuben, his first son. And then came Simeon, Levi, and Judah.

To Rachel's sorrow she seemed unable to bear children. Sorrow and humiliation it was, for in those days if a woman was barren it was considered to be her fault. So, according to the custom of the time she sent her maid servant, Bilhah, to Jacob to have children for her, and Bilhah bore Dan and Naphtali. Then Leah, thinking that she was through childbearing, sent her maid servant, Zilpah, in to Jacob, and she bore Gad and Asher. Then Leah conceived again, and bore Issachar and Zebulun, and then her only daughter, Dinah. And then, at last, Rachel conceived, and gave birth to Joseph. And, in the end, to Benjamin. Reuben, Simeon, Levi, Judah, Dan, Naphtali, Gad, Asher, Issachar, Zebulun, (Dinah), Joseph, and Benjamin. And of all the brothers it is Joseph, the penultimate son, whose story we know best.

Joseph's story starts with dissension. He brags of his dreams and infuriates his brothers. Then, when he is seventeen, he is out feeding his father's flocks, as David was to do many generations later. Joseph was with his brothers, Dan and Naphtali, who were Bilhah's sons, and with Gad and Asher, who were Zilpah's sons. Bilhah was Rachel's maid, and Zilpah was Leah's maid, and the sons of the two maids may have been made to feel inferior to the sons of the wives.

Joseph left the sons of the maids, and went to his father with *an evil report*. In the southern United States this would be called "bad-mouthing," and in checking several Bible translations I have not found out exactly who was bad-mouthing whom, or what the evil report was. But someone was the teller of ill tales, and this never brings good.

But Joseph, the favoured one, went tattling to his father, for Jacob *loved Joseph more than all his children, be-*

*cause he was the son of his old age, and he made him a coat of
many colours.*

What about little Benjamin? Was he too poignant a
reminder of Rachel's death?

A family of twelve or thirteen children used to be
commonplace. It is not, nowadays (though there have
been times when I have felt that there are at least that
many in our family). A family that size is a community in
itself. Almost all human needs can be met within the
family group.

The people who built Crosswicks, the old house my
husband and I loved and lived in for so many years, and
where we raised our children, could live off the less-than-
one-hundred acres that made up their dairy farm. Two
hundred plus years ago they grew all their own food,
eating from the garden and from the herd. They made
their own soap and candles, wove their own cloth. In the
close-knit community of the village of Goshen, what one
family did not produce, a neighbour did. In a much
smaller and more trivial way, Hugh never planted zuc-
chini or squash, knowing that we would get the overflow
from our neighbours.

Today, with farms being broken up, many being sold
for housing developments or condos, with more and
more people working, if not living, in cities, the family is
now what is called "nuclear." The larger family of uncles
and aunts and cousins is often a continent away, and so
the grouping of community is necessarily different.
Sometimes it is the people on the block. Or in the
development. In a small village it is the nearest neighbours and the community of the church.

My mother, growing up in a southern town, was surrounded by uncles and aunts and cousins. At the four

corners of St. John's Episcopal Church lived four great uncles. Almost all my mother's friends were cousins.

My mother-in-law lived in a southwestern city—a new city in a new state—where the people in the neighbourhood were divided into the Baptist families, the Methodist families, the Presbyterian families. At a further remove were the Episcopalian families. Further out yet, the Roman Catholic families. And, almost on another planet, the Jewish families.

This artificial barrier of culture and religion and race was at least lowered when a Jewish woman came to spend the High Holy Days at my Baptist parents-in-law's house, since she had to be able to walk to the synagogue and could not take public transportation or drive during those special days. This became a yearly occurrence, and though the requirement seemed outlandish to my Baptist mother-in-law, the two women became, in their own way, friends, able to share stories of children and child-raising, to swap recipes. There was at least as much to bring them together as to separate them, which seems to have been a salutary surprise to them both.

And whose God was more real? Did they not both worship the "God of Abraham, Isaac, and Jacob?" How essentially different were their Gods? This is a question I do not presume to answer. In Psalm 50, we are warned not to think that God is like us: *You thought wickedly, that I am like you, but I will reprove you.*

God reproves us whenever we decide that El is like us, or like our own particular group. There is only one criterion to use in deciding whether or not the image of God we are finding within us is really God's image, or a projection of ourselves. The one thing we know about God for certain is that *God is love.* Where there is not love, even if there is righteousness, or justice, it is not God.

This is perhaps the most difficult lesson of all to learn. If we love God, then we must also love each other. Indeed it would be a good and joyful thing if all God's children could learn to dwell together in unity.

Can the heavenly kingdom come until this happens? Joseph's relationships with his brothers are an example of disunity, and there would be no rest in Joseph's heart until at last there was reconciliation.

Reuben was the eldest of the twelve sons, and the one most interested in reconciliation. But he was not favoured.

Reuben

I was never anybody's favourite. Elder sons tend not to fare well in my genealogy, despite the emphasis on primogeniture. Cain killed his younger brother and is not likely to be forgotten for it. Ishmael was sent into exile, leaving the favoured younger brother, Isaac, at home. Of my Grandfather Isaac's two sons, my father, Jacob, the younger son, got all the plums. And there's an old story of a younger son who took all his share of his father's money and squandered it on women and riotous living, and yet, when he hit the bottom, and came home, his father gave a big party, and the elder brother went out and sulked. It is not an advantage to be the first-born.

And I was a disappointment to my mother, Leah, who had hoped that when she gave my father a son he would come to love her. But he had eyes only for the younger sister (the younger, again!) Rachel, the beauty, and the clever one. My mother was loving, and tender-eyed, and wouldn't have been considered bad-looking if she hadn't always been compared to Rachel.

It wasn't that my father disliked me. He was pleased to have a son. But my mother was Leah, not his adored Rachel, and my birth didn't turn his—well, fondness is the best I can call it—for Leah into love. I was a disappointment all round.

So were my mother's next three sons, though her fourth-born, Judah, ended up doing pretty well for himself. We four were fairly close in age, and we played together a lot, quarreled, hit each other in anger, and stood up for each other whenever anybody criticized us.

But none of us made our mother truly happy because our births didn't change anything between her and our father. On the other hand, our Aunt Rachel was jealous because our mother, Leah, had babies, and she was barren. She was beautiful, oh, was our Aunt Rachel ever beautiful, and when I was little I would have liked to sit on her lap. But when I tried to climb up on her she pushed me away and burst into tears.

Our mother didn't conceive again immediately after her fourth son, Judah, was born, and she was still trying to get our father to love her. It was a long time before I understood that a man could go to a woman's tent, and do all the things done to a woman who is loved, without love being there. Our father tolerated our mother. Yes, he was even fond of her. But he did not love her. He loved Aunt Rachel.

And still Aunt Rachel did not conceive. So she sent her maid, Bilhah, in to our father, and Bilhah, too, gave him two sons, and still he was not satisfied.

So my mother, Leah, sent her maid, Zilpah, in to our father, to give him more sons. Zilpah, in her own foreign way, was beautiful, so our father had no objection, and she gave him two more sons. What a passion he had for sons!

I was quite a big boy when one day I came across some mandrakes. Mandrakes are a plant shaped like a human man's body, and have magical powers, so I brought them to my mother, thinking to please her. If she wanted our father, Jacob, to love her, I wanted her to love me. Neither of us was very successful.

But she was pleased with the mandrakes, if not with me, but then Aunt Rachel saw the mandrakes and wanted them, and my mother and my aunt had one of their quarrels. But my mother kept the mandrakes, and my father came in to her that night, and she conceived and had another son, and then yet another, and then our little sister, Dinah, who was beautiful and loving. I was her big brother, her biggest brother, and at last somebody loved me, really loved me. I would carry her about on my shoulders, as soon as she was big enough, and throw her into the air and catch her, and she would shriek with terror and joy and cry, "Again! Again!"

Not that there was much time to play. We all worked hard, tending the land, the flocks of camels and sheep and goats. We lived with our Grandfather Laban, our mother's and Aunt Rachel's father. Laban's land was our home. We were all born there, and I think he regarded us as his sons.

One day we saw Aunt Rachel looking as though she'd walked out of the sunrise. At last she was pregnant, and had a son, Joseph. You should have seen our father. Lambs were roasted. Wine skins were emptied. You'd have thought he'd never had a son before. You'd have thought the ten of us meant nothing to him at all.

I tried to talk to my mother, but she sent me off to take care of my two youngest brothers—not precious Joseph, of course, but my mother's two youngest.

But Zilpah was taking care of them. It was her job, not mine, anyhow. Bilhah saw me and asked what was the matter.

I told her.

Bilhah was always kind to me, kinder than any of the other women. She took my face in her hands and looked at me with her gentle, deep eyes, blue as dawn. "You're nearly a man now, Reuben," she said. "If your father is to love you, he will love you for what you do as a man. Let him have pleasure in this new baby. Now he has eleven sons and a daughter and I hope he is satisfied." She dropped her hands from my face. "You're a handsome youth, Reuben. And you're kind. You're much the biggest and the strongest, but you never hurt the younger ones. You're never mean. One day you will make a woman happy. Don't fret about the way things are now. It will pass."

I had always loved Bilhah, fairer even than Zilpah, with hair that reached almost to her knees.

When I was younger and fell and scraped my knees it was only Bilhah who paid any attention. Zilpah, my mother's maid, knew that my mother did not love me because my birth had not made her find favour in my father's eyes, so she pushed me away. But Bilhah would wipe away my tears and kiss my hurt to make it better.

If I had a nightmare and woke up screaming, it was Bilhah who came hurrying through the night to comfort me, who stroked my forehead until I stopped being afraid and could go back to sleep.

One evening, after I had found the mandrakes and given them to my mother and so, inadvertently, been the cause of yet two more brothers, I followed Bilhah as she left the noisy cluster of tents. I watched her as she passed the place where the animals were tethered, stroking the mangy-looking camel she usually rode, and giving it a handful of mashed lentils. Then she headed for a sandy hill with palmettos and tawny grasses blowing in the desert wind. She sat down, digging her toes into the sand and putting her head down on her knees so that her hair fell about her like a golden curtain. With one hand she picked up some sand and let it dribble out of her fingers.

Bilhah wanted to be alone, and so did I, but I felt I could be alone better with Bilhah. I made a noise so that I wouldn't surprise her, approached her, and sat down beside her. She smiled at me, sidewise, without lifting her head, pushing her hair away from her face. Without thinking I raised my hand and stroked her hair, feeling the fine silkiness, soft as rain. To my surprise a great shudder ran through her, and I drew away before she did.

"You grow into a handsome man, my Reuben," she said.

I touched my upper lip and chin where curling hair was beginning to grow.

She stood up, slowly, gracefully, stretching her arms starwards. "I must go tend to little Joseph or my mistress will be angry."

Why was it that both my mother and my Aunt Rachel were far more demanding of Zilpah and Bilhah after they had given my father man-children than they had been before?

It came to pass that my father and my Grandfather Laban parted company over some striped and speckled cattle, and my father packed up all our tents and all our goods and took all our animals and ran off to the hill country of Gilead, where there was to be no balm for me.

Grandfather Laban found us there, and he and my father shouted at each other, and the little children all huddled in the tents. But my father and grandfather made up, hugging and kissing each other, and we set off again, heading towards Mamre, where my Grandfather Isaac, my father's father, whom I had never seen, had his tents.

I had spent my entire life in one place, on Grandfather Laban's land, going no further from home than to tend the flocks. And now we were on a journey across alien lands, to a place and people I had never seen.

It was a terrible journey.

We came to the land of the Hivites, in Canaan, and Dinah, our sister, but no longer our *little* sister, went out to visit the women of the land.

Dinah, I was beginning to realize, was far more beautiful than our mother, easily as beautiful as Aunt Rachel, and looked, in fact, more like her daughter than our mother's. This displeased our mother. I suspect it equally displeased Aunt Rachel.

Bilhah said to me, "It is hard on your mother, to be surpassed first by her sister and now by her daughter."

And by you, too, Bilhah—I thought, but did not say it.

Dinah met the young prince of that land, Shechem, and they lay together before betrothal, which is against all our customs. Some of my brothers said that he seized her against her will, and defiled her. To lie with a man before betrothal is, of course, defiling, but I do not believe it was against her will.

Prince Shechem was not only honourable, he was wild to marry Dinah, willing to do anything to have her as his wife. She was the sun and the moon and the stars to him.

34

My brothers Simeon and Levi, next to me in line, said that she had been disgraced. "Should our sister be treated like a whore?" they demanded.

They were very loud. They did not listen to Dinah. They did not listen to me, although I was the eldest.

Prince Shechem, and Hamor, his father, showed us great hospitality, offering us their land, suggesting that we marry their daughters, and it was apparent that Shechem was utterly dazzled by Dinah. He readily agreed to Simeon's and Levi's suggestion that he and all of the men of their tribe be circumcised, according to our custom, if that was what we wanted, before he married Dinah.

And then, when Shechem and all the men of that place were weak and sore from circumcision, my brothers Simeon and Levi slaughtered Shechem, and his father, Hamor, and all the Hivites. It was to avenge Dinah's honour, they said, but they also took all the gold and earrings and jewels they could lay their hands on.

And Dinah screamed and screamed and clawed at them but could not stop them, and she flung herself upon the body of Shechem and was covered with his blood.

"Defiled!" Simeon and Levi shouted. I picked Dinah up in my arms, her poor bloody young body quivering like a plucked bow string, and Bilhah and Zilpah and our mother took her away.

We had to flee that place. My father made everybody give back all the gold and earrings and jewels they had taken. If Simeon and Levi were the killers, the others lost no time in scavenging from the dead. Ah, God, what an un-human lot we were! My father hid all the loot under an oak, and we took up our tents in haste and got on our camels and left.

Who were Simeon and Levi to take the honour of Dinah onto their shoulders without consulting with me, the eldest?

I never wanted to see blood again.

So we went our way, with Bilhah and Zilpah trying to clean Shechem's blood from Dinah, who had stopped screaming, and had become silent and still as a stone. Simeon and Levi rode together, whispering. And our father turned his back on all of us except Aunt Rachel.

El. It was a sad journey.

When we came to Bethel, Aunt Rachel's old nurse, Deborah, died, and was buried there. Aunt Rachel wept and wept. She was heavy with child and had counted on her nurse to assist in the delivery.

Why did Deborah, with all her skill, have to die just then? Was the journey too hard for her old bones, the assassination of Shechem and all his people too shocking, Dinah's grief more than she could bear?

Aunt Rachel started her labour and we stopped and pitched the tents when we were still some distance from Ephrath. It was a hard labour, and all the women were in the tent with her to help with the delivery, and there was no Deborah to clear them away and give Aunt Rachel space to breathe, and none had the skill of Deborah, and suddenly Aunt Rachel screamed, as Dinah had screamed when Shechem was slaughtered before her eyes, and then there was a long and terribly empty silence broken, at last, by a baby's cry. And then there was laughter and joy and then silence again, a long silence. And then much sobbing from the women.

Bilhah came out of the tent, carrying a swaddled baby to give to our father.

It was Leah, my mother, who had to tell him that Rachel was dead.

It was a journey of storms and tears, and I longed for home and the land around Grandfather Laban's tents where I had been born and brought up. I knew that Grandfather Isaac was very old, and wondered if we'd make it to his tents before he died.

We buried Aunt Rachel and set up a pillar of stones upon her grave, and then we journeyed on, because there seemed nothing else to do, and pitched our tents beyond the tower of Eder.

My soul was dark. Our father mourned and groaned in grief. Dinah was still as stone, except when she took care of the baby, Benjamin, whose birthing had killed his mother, and I wondered if Benjamin would pull Dinah out of the frozen darkness into which she had been plunged since Shechem's murder. Simeon and Levi kept away from me and that was just as well.

I went into the tent where Bilhah was, combing her moon-bright hair. Her breasts were like roses. She looked at me, and her eyes were pools of calm. She opened her arms and I moved to her and into her and knew her.

I knew her.

And I felt loved. For the first time in my life I felt loved in a way that was very different from Dinah's baby love of me. El, it was good.

I was too drowned in love to hear the tent flap lifted, but someone must have peered in, because whoever that someone was told our father what I had done. What Bilhah and I had done.

If Dinah broke a taboo in letting Shechem come in to her before they were married, I broke an equally rigid one by sleeping with my father's concubine. At least he paid attention to me for awhile, the first time he had ever done that, even if it was to berate me. He was still mad with grief for Rachel and hardly knew what he was saying.

I left him and went to the tent where Dinah was sitting on the camel's furniture, rocking our baby brother, Benjamin.

"I paid, Reuben," she whispered, "and so will you."

I left her with the baby. I wanted to go to Bilhah, regardless of my father's wrath, but she shook her head.

"No, my Reuben. It will only bring more trouble."

I did not go in to her. There was trouble anyhow.

Simeon and Levi

are brethren; instruments of cruelty are in their habitations.

O my soul, come not thou into their secret; unto their assembly, mine honour, be not thou united: for in their anger they slew a man, and in their selfwill they digged down a wall.

Cursed be their anger, for it was fierce; and their wrath, for it was cruel: I will divide them in Jacob, and scatter them in Israel.

Genesis 49:5-7

Simeon

2

SIMEON AND LEVI sulked because they were not praised for avenging Dinah's honour. It was a time of trouble and it was a time of grief. Reuben grieved. Bilhah grieved. They were a large group traveling to Mamre to find Isaac, but their grief was solitary. Jacob kept apart, angry with all his sons—except Joseph. Reuben and Judah walked together, not talking. Dinah was white and silent as a stone. Simeon blamed Levi, and Levi blamed Simeon. Only Rachel, her pregnancy blooming, smiled as she rode along on her donkey. They were all together, but all more separate than they had ever been before.

So was I. After Hugh's death the phone rang constantly. Mail poured in. I was surrounded by love. But my grief itself was still solitary.

I kept to my lecturing schedule because that was what Hugh would have wanted me to do, going, the first month, from Portland, Maine to Denver, Colorado. In Portland it was the phone that almost undid me, looking at the phone and knowing that I couldn't pick it up and call Hugh to tell him that I'd arrived safely. But the work went well. I wrote in my journal, "Both yesterday and today the response was warm and generous. In a way, when people expect me to be 'good' they do half the work for me."

After Hugh's death Crosswicks was my base while I struggled to learn about grief, to learn to live with loss, drawing strength from the ancient hills. I knew that I would be moving back to my apartment in New York after Christmas, where my granddaughter, Charlotte, was living with one of her classmates. But for those first months I needed to be at Crosswicks, to feel a part of the rhythm of the land, the turning of the season, the coming of winter and snow and short days and long nights. The first weeks of grief are weeks when one is in shock. I functioned, kept my lecturing schedule. I think I functioned moderately well, but I was, as it were, on automatic pilot.

Christmas was at Crosswicks, with family and friends to surround me with warmth, and then I moved back to our (yes, in my mind, still Hugh's and mine) apartment on the upper west side of New York. How very blessed I was to have Charlotte and her classmate living with me. And Léna, Charlotte's fourteen-month-older sister, was just a few blocks away in a Barnard dorm, and the girls, by their very existence, kept me in life. Charlotte's and Léna's parents had moved from New York to San Francisco the year before, where Alan is dean of Episcopal Grace Cathedral, and his and Josephine's distance is made bearable by Charlotte's and Léna's closeness to me. It also meant that my children didn't have to worry about my moving back alone to an apartment I had shared with Hugh for so many years.

Jacob took his tent with him wherever he went. He was always, therefore, "home." I had to make the move from Crosswicks to the apartment in Manhattan. I wrote, "Despite the visibility of two college students the apartment is very strange without Hugh. I am not sure where I am going to sleep tonight. I had thought the back room with my desk, but I'm inclining more and more to our own bed. We'll see." "Our own bed" it was, the king-size bed Hugh and I had bought together while we were still living at Crosswicks. Both boxspring and mattress are worn and old enough to need replacing. But not quite yet.

The Colorado trip was for a group of Christian writers gathered together by Richard Foster. Most of the writers I knew and respected; many were already my friends. But that first night I said firmly, "I am not a Christian writer. I am a writer who is a Christian." There is a big difference. Journal: " 'Christian' writing still makes me irritable, because a 'Christian' writer does not necessarily have to be a good writer, and so does not have to serve the work." And, as I understand the Gospel, the Good News is to be spread, not kept for the in-group who already have it.

Again, I wrote in my journal: "Night before last I dreamed that I was on a freighter-sized boat, and Michael [one of Hugh's doctors] was the captain. He explained that he captained a ship half the time in order to be an oncologist the other half.

"Last night I dreamed that Hugh was being given a transfusion, but the visual part of the dream was not Hugh, but the crumply, dark red, plastic transfusion bags. Mostly I haven't been remembering my dreams this summer—and why am I still calling it 'this summer' when not only is there snow on the ground here, but summer is fully over and the trees fast losing their leaves in northwest Connecticut?"

And then, "Last Sunday or Monday morning Clyde Kilby died, simply, quietly, in his sleep. Martha went to wake him with a kiss and lo, he was dead. A terrible shock for her, but how good for Clyde, past his mid-eighties, with lung problems which could have given him a suffocating death." Clyde Kilby, a dear friend, the person responsible for the wonderful collection at Wheaton College of the papers of C.S. Lewis, George Macdonald, Tolkien, G.K. Chesterton, Dorothy Sayers, among others. The person responsible for my own papers going to Wheaton Library's Special Collection. Clyde, gone from us. Another in a long line of griefs, though Clyde, like the patriarchs, died *full of years*.

"Friday night towards morning I slipped into sleep and dreamed that Hugh and I were driving along a country road at night and I thought that the doctors were wrong, that he was in remission, that he was going to be all right. Then I felt something warm and wet, and realized blood was flowing from him, and said, 'Darling, are you all right?' and realized that his life blood was flowing from him, and reached over to grab the wheel. It was the first time I have dreamed about him and was, I suppose, a dream of acceptance of his death."

But later that day I wrote, "And yet today I am incredulous. It is not possible that Hugh is gone, that if I play the piano he won't come in to me at seven with ice clinking in a glass, that he won't come out to the kitchen to talk while I make dinner, cutting up celery and tomatoes and lettuce and other goodies to fix the salad. That we won't travel together, give readings together. No, it is incredible."

At my next job I went to dinner with a group of librarians and was asked what my life is like, "And I had to say that I don't know, that without Hugh it is going to be very different. Lecture trips like this give it a kind of consistency. I was thinking last night as I got into bed that I have done this same bed-time routine many a time after a lecture, so it is familiar and comfortable. The only difference is that I can't pick up the phone and hear Hugh's voice on the other end of the wire."

Moving back to the apartment was difficult. Simeon felt displaced picking up his tent and moving from Grandfather Laban's land. I felt displaced in my own apartment. In order to have my desk in my bedroom, which was essential with the girls in the other two rooms, I had to get rid of the king-size bed. Our building was covered with scaffolding, as it had been for over four years, with the old stonework all being pointed, which hadn't been done since the apartment was built in 1912. Hugh and I had planned to redecorate as soon as the scaffolding came down. Now I would have to do it alone—but the scaffolding was still up. I moved the guest room bed and my desk into Hugh's and my bedroom with the help of young friends who did all the physical labour.

The scaffolding remained, but old traditions were gone forever. New ones came in to take their place. One evening I wanted to have some friends in for dinner. So did the girls. So we had a combined dinner party. To my joy the girls loved this chronological mix, and we got in the habit of multi-generational dinner parties, assembling together as many decades as possible. As has always been my bargain, I did the cooking, and the girls cleaned up. I'll cook for almost any number (my record as of now is fifty-eight) as long as the kitchen is taken care of after dinner.

How wonderful it is for me to have these splendid young women doing a good job of "bringing me up."

What would have happened to Jacob after Rachel's death if he hadn't had the support of and the responsibility for his large family?

My granddaughters and their friends keep me in the midst of things, help me to live in the chaos that comes when we rearrange beds and desks, and try to clean and polish the old apartment.

Jacob didn't have any such citified problems. His home was his tent wherever it was pitched. He had no phone. No warm bathtub in which to relax and ease sore muscles. No beds with sheets and blankets. What must the smell have been like?

But grief is grief, in the desert, in the city, in a tent or in a hotel.

And Jacob came to his father in Mamre, where Abraham and Isaac sojourned. And Isaac was a hundred and eighty years old. And Isaac gave up the ghost and died, and was gathered unto his people, being old and full of days, and his sons Esau and Jacob buried him. And Jacob dwelt in the land where his father was a stranger, in the land of Canaan.

Another death, another grief. But Jacob and his family settled down in Canaan, and there the younger children, Joseph and Benjamin, grew up. It was home to them, as Grandfather Laban's land had been to the others.

One day Jacob asked Joseph to go check on his brothers who were tending their father's flock in Shechem.

Where? I thought, startled as I read that. Yes, it appears to be the same place where Simeon and Levi murdered young Shechem, the prince of that land. There are many things in Scripture that are not to be understood, perhaps because so many years have passed that things have been left out, or added to, or shifted around. Or perhaps we are simply expected to understand, as Jesus expected his listeners to understand when he referred to passages in the Old Testament.

Joseph went to do his father's bidding, but he could not find his brothers. *A man asked him, "What are you looking for?"*

And he said, "I'm looking for my brothers. Do you know where they're feeding their flocks?" And the man said, "They've left here. I heard them say, 'Let's go to Dothan.'" So Joseph went after his brothers and found them in Dothan.

And when they saw him from a distance, before he came near them, they conspired together to slay him. And they said to one another, "Behold, here comes the dreamer. Let us slay him and cast him into some pit, and we will say, 'Some evil beast has devoured him, and we shall see what will become of his dreams.' "

When Reuben heard this he was deeply disturbed. Was more murder going to be piled on top of the murder of Shechem and his people? He said, *"Shed no blood, but cast him into this pit that is in the wilderness, and lay no hand on him."* Reuben's plan was to rescue his brother from the pit later, and return him to his father.

We are not told which of Joseph's brothers were in on the conspiracy to kill him. It is easy to suspect Simeon and Levi who were already killers, and perhaps the place itself reminded them of murder: Shechem. But only Reuben opposed them. Surely the sons of the two maids would have been jealous of Jacob's rank favouritism of Rachel's son. Benjamin was too young to have been with the older brothers, wandering with their flocks far from their home tents to find fresh pasture.

There seems to have been little discussion about whether or not to kill Joseph. Only Reuben pulled back in horror. Surely we should remember him well because he tried to save the adolescent boy. But when it came time for the ancient Jacob to give his blessing to his sons, Reuben still had to pay for having gone in to Bilhah, Rachel's maid, Jacob's concubine. A taboo broken is a taboo broken, and throughout the legends of many cultures this appears an implacable law: break the taboo, and no matter how ignorant you are, no matter whether or not the taboo was broken inadvertently, whether or not you meant well, retribution will surely follow.

So Reuben was to suffer.

It happened that *when Joseph reached his brothers, they stripped him out of his coat, his coat of many colours that he wore, and they took him, and cast him into a pit; the pit was empty; there was no water in it.*

They sat down to eat bread, and looked up, and saw a company of Ishmaelites coming from Gilead with their camels, bearing spices and balm and myrrh, on their way to carry it all to Egypt.

The Ishmaelites, descendants of their Grandfather Isaac's half-brother, Ishmael. It was a small world. Wherever you turned you were apt to encounter at least a distant cousin.

Judah, Leah's fourth son, the younger brother of Simeon and Levi who slaughtered Shechem, *said to his brothers, "What profit is it to us if we slay our brother and conceal his blood? Come, let us sell him to the Ishmaelites, and let not our hand be upon him, for he is our brother, and our flesh."* Judah's suggestion was pragmatic rather than compassionate.

And his brethren were content. Then the Midianite merchants came by, and the brothers drew and lifted Joseph up out of the pit, and sold Joseph to the Ishmaelites for twenty pieces of silver, and they took him with them to Egypt.

Where was Reuben during this transaction? The next verse of Scripture says, *And Reuben returned to the pit, and behold, Joseph was not in the pit, and Reuben rent his clothes. And he returned to his brothers and said, "The child is not! And I, where shall I go?"*

The other brothers paid little attention to Reuben's anguish. The next verse is: *And they took Joseph's coat, and killed a kid from their flock of goats, and dipped the coat in the blood. And they took the coat of many colours and brought it to their father, and said, "This we have found. Tell us whether it is your son's coat or not."*

And Jacob knew it and said, "It is my son's coat. An evil beast has devoured him. Joseph is without doubt rent in pieces."

And Jacob rent his clothes (as Reuben had done) *and put on sack cloth and mourned for his son many days.*

He would not be comforted, but said, "I will go down into the grave mourning for my son." And his father wept for him.

It is not a pretty story, but we are so over-familiar with it that repetition has blunted the ugliness of what the brothers did. Joseph was a spoiled adolescent; they had cause to be jealous, but not cause to do what they did. And had it not been for Reuben and Judah, they would certainly have had Joseph's blood on their hands. Had they forgotten Cain?

What a rude awakening for young Joseph. Had he suspected the depths of his older brothers' resentment? What a shock to the pampered adolescent, first to be flung into a pit, then to be sold into the hand of strangers. Who kept the money?

Sometimes terrible things are redeemed in unexpected ways. This sudden and violent separation from everything known and loved and familiar was the beginning of Joseph's growing-up. This beginning of the breaking of the pampered pet was essential to his development into a mature human being. Likely the Ishmaelites were rough with him. He was, after all, a purchase, a commercial property, and that made him a slave. At least his life was spared.

But to Jacob, to the women, Joseph was dead. Now a new and terrible grief was added to Jacob's grief over Rachel. In my journal I wrote, "Grief is different from unhappiness. In unhappiness one is stuck in time. In grief time is totally askew. Christmas at Crosswicks was only three days ago and it was years ago. Coming to Maplewood to Maria and John and the babies is a parenthesis in time. . . . It is time I started saying 'this winter' and stopped saying 'this summer.' 'This summer' was so fiercely intense it's hard to get out of its grip. Especially since *out of its grip* means *out of my life with Hugh* and into a new life where I'm still groping my way."

So Jacob, too, because of Joseph's death, moved into a new way of loss. How could his other sons comfort him? Did he turn to little Benjamin?

The older brothers carried the burden of what they had done, but how painfully it weighted their consciences we do not know. Reuben, it would seem, was filled with pain and regret for having failed to rescue Joseph and return him to his father. The others may have felt that they were fine fellows for having spared the braggart's life, for having sold him into Egypt rather than murdering him. In any case, life had to go on, there was work to do, flocks to tend.

And where was God, the Maker of the Universe who took Abraham out to ask him if he could count the stars, who sent the ram in the bush to spare Isaac, who wrestled with Jacob, during all this? Thoughts of God seem to be singularly absent in Jacob's sons, and if there is any sense of God at all it is the tribal god, the one god among many gods, the masculine deity who is around to help his tribe. To the casual reader this rather chauvinist figure appears to be the God of the Old Testament. Our visions of God are partial and incomplete at best. But the God who shines through the Old Testament is the mighty Creator who made the brilliance of all those stars he showed Abraham, the God of the universe.

There have been many times in history when people must have wondered what kind of God we Christians have—for instance, when crusaders slaughtered Orthodox Christians in Constantinople; when the Spanish Inquisitors burned people at the stake for tiny differences in interpretation of faith; in Salem where a woman could be hanged as a witch if an angry neighbour accused her out of spite. Perhaps God needs less of our fierce protectiveness for his cause, and more of our love to El, to each other.

Did Simeon and Levi think they were doing God's will when they slaughtered Shechem? Did the brothers even consider what God would think of their selling Joseph into Egypt?

Did Reuben turn over his anguish to God when he was unable to save his brother? Perhaps he wanted to unburden himself to Bilhah, but whenever he even turned in the direction of Bilhah's tent his father's suspicious eyes were fixed on him. Bilhah's consolations were denied him forever.

Bilhah

There are advantages to being a woman and a slave, a foreigner with gentler gods than the harsh man-god of my mistress, a warrior god who helped them slaughter my people, take over our land, leaving the ground slippery with blood lapped up by their wild dogs.

Those few of us who were left were taken into captivity, and because I was young, my courses having started only a few moons before, and comely, I was chosen to be a slave girl for the master's favoured wife. Not much older than I am is she, and beautiful, with heavy curling hair the colour of dark honey, and amber eyes made darker by the long black fringe of her lashes. She treats me kindly, if casually, and I am no cause of jealousy to her; my own beauty, prized by my tribe, not being as appealing to the men who killed my father and brothers as to those slain men who were dazzled by my pale curtain of hair bright against copper skin, my firm young breasts, and long straight thighs.

It has not been bad here. There are servants under me, not slaves, yet less free than I, who must do my bidding or feel the lash, though I discourage that.

No whip has touched me in my long years among these strange people. And I have had hours of precious solitude, particularly during those two nine-moons when my body held my master's sons.

Ish, how she wept, my mistress, she, the younger, the more beautiful, the more desired of the two sisters. But it was the elder one, with her strange eyes looking in different directions so that you never knew what she was seeing, who gave birth to sons.

My mistress sent me to the master to have sons for her. The custom was strange to me. But she explained how the master's grandfather, one Abraham, had had his first son by his wife's maid, and that it was the way of their people. The master took me moderately kindly, for if my fair beauty is strange to these rough people my body can still awaken desire. He was gentle, but quick. And when my body filled with his child I was given milk of goat and camel to drink, allowed to stay away from the cook tent with its rank smells of oil and garlic, given whatever I asked for to eat, the fruits of home, pomegranate and wild pear.

The birthing times, especially the first, were beyond my comprehension. The midwives were there, the most skilled my mistress's old nurse. I longed simply to squat, with one woman of my tribe experienced in deliveries to urge me along. But no, my mistress was there, trying to make her body part of mine, and when, after the hours of anguish, the child burst forth she claimed it as her own.

Strange people. Strange customs. However, it was my breasts that had the milk, and I was allowed the child at feeding times, allowed, too, to keep him clean, then hand his tiny perfection back to waiting Rachel.

Twice I did this for her, twice bore sons in her place, willing because she was kind and full of sorrow and shame, because Jacob was a fair lover, and because I enjoyed the freedom from the heavier burdens, freedom to take time to think what it means to be a woman.

If I had the choice, would I be a man in this strange tribe whose god is a man, rough and wild, leaping on my master in the dark and striking him on the thigh so that he limps, and will forever move that one leg with difficulty and pain?

My goddess does not come so close, though she, too, is wild, as are the deities of all the tribes. The goddess orders the courses of the moon as well as women, and the turning of the seasons and the tides tells us when to sow and when to harvest, when to plant and when to lie fallow. Tells the women to rejoice in our slender wrists which, no matter how much we labour in the fields, will never be as strong as a man's, but are more deft and delicate.

When we are children we play together, boy and girl, not paying attention to our differences which are merely genital. Our bodies for the first years are otherwise indistinguishable. Then what hardens in the boys softens in the girls. Our breasts bloom like small flowers and our hips curve into roundness. We can no longer run as far or jump as high, or wrestle friend or brother to the ground, though we may try, unwilling to give up our wild freedom, even after we have become women.

But we and the boys are no longer the same. The difference used to be no more than a matter of standing or squatting to let out our water. Now our women's bodies are warm and full like new wineskins. And when they empty of a child, our breasts in turn are full, bursting with milk. When the child can toddle, our hips are small shelves on which we carry them, sitting astride us in comfort. Let a man try to hold a child this way and it slides down his thigh.

There are tribes where women proclaim themselves to be the same as men, sit astride wild horses, throw spears, gnaw meat off bones. Their hair is full of lice. They stink, and yet the stink is not a man's. It is folly, I think, for a woman to try to be a man.

And why? When I was a child it was the women who were wise. The oldest ones could listen to the goddess in the moon, the angels in the stars, listen well enough to warn us of earthquake or of drought. It was the old wise women who were heeded, honoured by the men. When a child was born, male or female, it was not merely a source of pride for the man or prestige for the woman but of joy for us all, and the goddess laughed her pleasure with us.

Here my sons were hardly mine once they were weaned, but possessions of Jacob's pride. Even after Rachel had a child of her own my sons were still more hers than mine.

Sons. How greedy Jacob was for sons! Leah with her strange eyes, gave him four. Then her maid, Zilpah, gave her two more to add to Jacob's quiver, and then Leah filled it further, with two more sons and a daughter.

I still remember how good it is to be a woman, to give an offering of love, as I gave to Reuben, Jacob's first son—to give, instead of being taken.

It is the calling of women to give. Men believe that it is their prerogative to take. I would rather be a giver than a taker.

If it is thought less to be a woman than a man, how can a woman give? It is in the nature of a woman to give love. Ish! Will I ever give again?

Levi

3

WHAT VISION DID LEVI HAVE of the universe? Was he awed by the magnificence of the stars at night? Or was he so tired by the day's work that he retreated to his tent? Certainly, if he thought about it at all, his understanding of the universe and his place in it was simpler than ours.

Simpler than ours. The planet was still sparsely populated. When flocks had eaten the pastureland bare, the nomadic Hebrews moved on to fresher fields, even if it meant pushing out people who were already there. But that was all right, because God wanted them, his people, to have the land, so the heathen didn't matter. *"He hath shewed his people the power of his works, that he may give them the heritage of the heathen."* Alas, these words of the psalmist have been behind our treatment of the native Americans, and England's Empire. Is this what God really wants?

But God, El, the God of Joseph and the Patriarchs, seems to be almost two separate gods, the tribal god whom Bilhah found so offensive, and who still offends many people today, and the God who was the Maker of the Universe, Creator of the Stars, the All in All, the God of Love who still lights our hearts.

The tribal god can be described and defined. The God of love, the God of beginnings, cannot. And we have the desire to define, to encompass, to understand with our minds, rather than our hearts, the God we proclaim.

For Joseph and his brothers, this little planet was, of course, the center of all things, with the stars glistening in the sky for our pleasure, the sun and the moon for our sole benefit. When the Creator had created the universe in a brilliant burst of love, had seen what had been made, he called it good, very good, but it had been assumed that nothing was really very important until God had achieved the pinnacle of Creation in the persons of two human beings, Adam and Eve.

This anthropic point of view continued, basically unchanged, until well into the Middle Ages. Even after the birth of Jesus most people saw the universe very much as Joseph and his brothers saw it, despite the fact that God had come to us as Jesus of Nazareth in the most extraordinary outpouring of love that can be imagined—though, alas, it *cannot* be imagined. How can we understand that God cared so much about this sorry planet that the Creator Elself came to visit? To be with us as the Lord Jesus who lived and died and rose for us? And then, after the Ascension we were sent the Holy Spirit to give us strength.

But as far as the physical understanding of the universe went, this planet was still the center of all things. Joseph in Egypt was able and willing to change his way of looking at the world. He may have been spoiled, but he was also bright and flexible. Throughout the centuries many individuals have been willing to be flexible, while their institutions have not. All institutions resist change, and whenever anything happens to alter what the institution has decided is the right picture of God and the universe—not only the right picture but the only picture—they resist. It is frightening to be told that the "truth" that the institution has been teaching is not the "truth" after all. But it isn't the truth that changes, only our knowledge. Truth is eternal, but our knowledge is always flawed and partial.

The way we look at the making of the universe is inevitably an *image*, an *icon*. Joseph, standing out in the desert at night and looking at the sun sliding down behind the western horizon, turning to see the moon coming up in the east, understandably saw the sun and the moon as heavenly bodies that revolved around the earth. That, indeed, is how it looks to all of us. We may know that it is not the sun that is setting, but rather our planet that is turning, nevertheless the evidence of our eyes is that *the sun sets*.

As our knowledge changes, our images, our icons, must change, too, or they become idols. Our understanding of the universe today is very different from Joseph's understanding, but we, too, must be willing to allow our understanding to change and grow as we learn more about God's glorious work. We still tend to cling to our own ideas, or what we have been taught, or told, and to feel threatened if anything new is revealed. What we know now is probably as far from the way God really created as the patriarch's limited vision and version. How do we stay open to revelation?

It must have been a cozy feeling to believe that the earth was Creation's center, with everything else revolving around it for our pleasure. The self-satisfied human ego got a terrible blow in the sixteenth century with the

Copernican Revolution which displaced earth as the center of the universe. But finally it had to be acknowledged that the sun, not the earth, was the center of the solar system, and that instead of the sun revolving around us, we revolve around the sun.

Human pride and self-satisfaction got yet another blow when it was seen that our sun is only one of many in our great galaxy the Milky Way—so gorgeous to look at when I am at Crosswicks, our house in the Litchfield hills, and I walk the dogs at night and see it flowing across the sky. I look up and try to understand that our solar system is a tiny pinprick in that great river of stars, and a relatively unimportant one in the exurbs of our spiral galaxy. It is the way we now understand God's Creation, but it is still only partial understanding. The truth I hold to is that it is all God's, joyfully created, and that it is good.

After it had been accepted that our planet was part of a solar system in the Milky Way, then came the even more humbling realization that the Milky Way itself is not unique, but is an ordinary spiral galaxy among hundreds of billions of galaxies all rushing away from each other to the distant reaches of space.

It was no doubt a good thing for the human ego to learn about the immensity of the universe. And in this century we have discovered not only the vastness of the macrocosm, but the equal vastness of the microcosm, the almost unimaginably small world of sub-atomic particles. It gives some idea of the smallness when we realize that sub-atomic particles are as much smaller than we are as the galaxies are larger than we are.

But this knowledge also had the effect of making the thinking, questioning human creature seem pretty unimportant. Who are we that God should be mindful of us? Worse than that, to some people it seemed that we are

God's biggest mistake, with our unending wars, our terrorism, our greed which has caused us to be poor stewards of the land given us to nurture. How do we account for man's inhumanity to men? What has happened to God's image in us?

Even when we list our great saints and artists, Teresa, Julian of Norwich, Bach, Shakespeare, Rembrandt, nothing we do seems very important, set against the enormity of Creation.

The God I believe in is greater than anything I or anybody else can conceive. But part of my faith is that the Creator who made human beings with at least an iota of free will does not diminish that marvelous and terrible gift by manipulating us. God is not a Great Dictator. Every once in a while when life seems nearly unbearable I might long, fleetingly, for such a God who has already, as it were, written the story, but I do not want to be part of a tale that has already been told. God calls us to work with our Maker on the fulfilling of Creation. What we do either moves us towards the Second Coming, the reconciliation of all things, or holds us back.

Yes, each of us is that important, and this can be very frightening. With our abuse of free will we have increased the ravages of disease; our polluted planet is causing more people to die of cancer than when the skies and seas and earth were clean. But this does not mean that we have to throw out the idea of a God who loves and cares.

What kind of a God of love can we believe in at this point in the human endeavor? How do we reconcile God's love and the strange gift of free will?

As a human parent I have had to learn to allow my children to make their own mistakes, to become free adults and so, truly human. I cannot rush in and correct every error in judgment, or fix everything that goes wrong. The children of parents who attempt to do that usually end up as emotional cripples. The message of the Incarnation underlines the message that is all through Scripture: God cares about Creation. God is in it with us. If we hurt, God hurts.

If we abuse our free will, we hurt God. If we really cared about God and Creation, how could we continue to cut down the rain forests? to tear apart the ozone layer? to forget that our grandchildren will suffer from the results of our greed? What is happening to us human beings? Have all our icons become idols?

An icon is the opposite of an idol. An icon is an open window to the love of God. An idol is a closed door in the face of God's love. We must be sure that our symbols remain icons, rather than walls, like the Berlin Wall, or the Maginot Line, or the Iron Curtain—all of which have shown their fallibility.

Whenever we get too sure of ourselves we get a come-uppance. The Church Establishment stubbornly resisted giving up the Aristotelian idea that the earth is flat, with heaven above, hell below, a sort of cosmic sandwich. It was a blow to human pride to discover that the earth was not in fact a sandwich, but a slightly pear-shaped sphere. What did that do to the ideas of heaven and hell? It staggered some people for a while. Where, indeed, *are* heaven and hell? Have we been able to move beyond the literalism of the Middle Ages?

When Copernicus died in 1543 he had started what came to be known as the Copernican Revolution. This Polish doctor and church administrator displaced the earth as the center of the universe. Instead, from his observations he deduced that the earth is a planet, and this denigration of our place in the scheme of things was a bitter blow to human self-satisfaction. When Joseph dreamed of the sun and the moon and the eleven stars bowing down before him his cosmology was the old one of the earth as the center. But finally, in the sixteenth century, we had to acknowledge the falsity of the old image and adopt a new one.

What a terrible shock to the establishment that had taught its people that we are the center of everything and the reason for everything else! No wonder the Church went through the furious and futile process of denial. The closed, comfortable system had been burst asunder, and this produced anger and panic, rather than joy and wonder.

Giordano Bruno, one of Copernicus's disciples, shocked the establishment further when he conceived of the universe as infinite, and filled with countless stars which were suns. And then Johannes Kepler came up with the distressing realization that the orbits of the planets were not circles, but ellipses. The circle was considered perfect. How could planets travel a course that was less than perfect? What did this do to God, and Creation?

Nothing, of course, but we creatures have often confused protecting God with protecting our own ideas. We get frightened, and so we focus on peripheral ideas instead of on the glory of God and all that has been made. We cling to our untenable position and are afraid of changing it, unable to laugh at our grand statements and move on.

Throughout the centuries many grandiose statements have been made, both by scientists and theologians, yet most of these statements have had to be revised and expanded, if not discarded. How difficult it was for the

Church to let go the image of planet earth as the center of the universe! Now it no longer upsets most people that our planet is in an ordinary solar system in the Milky Way. The important thing is that we still belong to the One who created it all.

When Darwin's discoveries indicated that perhaps the world had taken more than seven earth days to make and that it was considerably older than anybody had expected, this shook many people so badly that they felt that they had to choose between God and evolution, with a terrible misunderstanding of the beautiful interdependence of religion and science. A while ago when I was at Berea College in Kentucky I was asked the usual earnest questions about creationism vs. evolution.

I laughed and said that I really couldn't get very excited about it. The only question worth asking is whether or not the universe is God's. If the answer is YES! then why get so excited about *how*? The important thing is that we are God's, created in love. And what about those seven days? In whose time are they? Eastern Standard Time? My daughter in San Francisco lives in a time zone three hours earlier than mine. In Australia, what time is it? Did God create in human time? Solar time? Galactic time? What about God's time? What matter if the first day took a few billennia in our time, and the second day a few billennia more?

I told the student at Berea that some form of evolution seems consistent with our present knowledge, and that I didn't think that God put the fossil skeletons of fish in the mountains of Nepal to test our faith, as some creationists teach. But if I should find out tomorrow that God's method of creation was something quite different from either creationism or evolution, that would in no way shake my faith, because that is not where my faith is centred.

Thank God. If my faith were based on anything so fragile, how would I have lived through my husband's dying and death? How would I continue to live a full and loving life? My faith is based on the wonder that everything is contained in the mind of God, all that we can see, all that we cannot see, all that is visible and all that—like sub-atomic particles—is invisible. All the laughter, all the pain, all the birthing and living and dying and glory, all our stories, without exception, are given dignity by God's awareness and concern.

But we get frightened, and we begin to wonder if all this explosion of knowledge doesn't make us so tiny and insignificant that we don't even count in the vastness of Creation. In the enormity of existence, we ask, Is there really a point to it all?

That there is, indeed, a point is something that all who believe in Christ affirm. We may not always know what the point is, but we base our lives on *God's* knowing. When we say that Christ is Lord we are affirming that God cares so much that we get the point, that the Second Person of the Trinity came to live with us, to be one of us, just to show us the point.

But we keep losing it. It's all too complex. Life is unjust. Illness and death strike seemingly at random. Our planet reels dizzily, rocked by war and suspicion and hate—hate like that of Levi for Shechem. How do we make any reasonable sense of the big things, the little things, of Levi slaughtering Shechem?

A flicker of understanding came to me many years ago when Hugh and I were living on a small dairy farm and raising our children. We went through several years when we, and the village, had more death and tragedy than is statistically normal. The theologians I was reading didn't help me, but the small community of our Congregational Church did. Anglican Madeleine and Baptist Hugh found a loving church home in the white spired church across the street from the General Store. But I was still asking a lot of big, cosmic questions to which I was finding no satisfactory answers.

Was it a coincidence that just as I was ready to start writing *A Wrinkle in Time* I came across a book of Einstein's and discovered the new physics? Einstein, with his theories of relativity, Planck, with his quantum theory, the astrophysicists and particle physicists opened for me a new world in which I glimpsed the glory of God.

I'm often asked about my great science background. My great science background is zilch. When I was in school and college the scientists were pretty arrogant. Adam's and Eve's eating of the fruit of the tree of the knowledge of good and evil was about to pay off. What we didn't know, we would know shortly. Most scientists found science and religion as irreconcilable as did most religionists. I took as little science as I possibly could. In high school I had to take chemistry in order to get into college. Our chemistry lab was an old greenhouse, and one day I was pretending I was Madame Curie and blew the place up. That was the most exciting thing that happened to me in chemistry. In college we had to take a science course, so I took psychology.

But then we penetrated to the heart of the atom and the scientists discovered that they really didn't know very much after all. For every question they answered, two more questions arose.

As I began to read more and more of the world of particle physics I found myself more and more willing to ask questions. I had been trying to understand and to define God and the marvelous mystery of the Incarnation with my intellect. But that doesn't work. The Incarnation is God's act of total love for us, but it is not to be understood as algebra is understood. It is in the realm of faith, and faith is not for the provable, but for that which is beyond proof.

I was nourished by the vision of the universe as being totally interrelated, with nothing happening in isolation. Everything affects everything else. *Ask not for whom the bell tolls. It tolls for thee.* Indeed, we live in a *uni*verse.

The theologians I was reading were not the right ones for me, with their proofs of the unprovable, their isolationism, their judgmentalism. Granted, I was reading the wrong theologians. But I began to find my theology in my reading of the physicists. These men and women, studying the makeup of the universe as it has developed through the billennia, see it as designed in such a way that life, sentient life, is inevitable, is part of a plan (God's plan), not an accidental occurrence in the development of our galaxy. Of course, we've known that all along, as have Bach and John the Evangelist and Lady Julian of Norwich and the other rejoicers, but it seems a new thought to the physicists. I'm pleased that they've caught up with it.

These ideas are beautifully expressed in one of my favourite hymns, an ancient one from the fourth century,

Of the father's love begotten
E'er the worlds began to be,
He is Alpha and Omega,

He the source, the ending he,
Of the things that are, that have been,
And that future years shall see,
Evermore and evermore.

John Wheeler, one of the important physicists of this
century, suggests that the principles of quantum
mechanics point to a need for the universe to produce a
phenomenon like us human creatures to observe and contemplate all that has been created.

To observe and to contemplate! Indeed, that seems as
much a theological as a scientific thought. The great mys-
tics throughout the centuries have been observers and
contemplators of God's glory. The psalmist asks in Psalm
113, *"Who is like our God?"* and it is answered, *"Who
humbles himself to behold (observe and contemplate) the things
that are in heaven and in the earth."* It takes humility for us
to stop and behold, to observe and contemplate.
Humility, and courage.

What we observe changes us, and we change what we
observe. I think of the game we used to play, of looking
steadily at someone's foot, in a classroom, on the subway.
After a short time the foot would begin to move.

The physicists tell us that objectivity is an illusion. We
cannot observe anything objectively, because to observe
something is to change it. And, often, to be changed.

So what does our calling to be observers and contemplators imply? Does the universe really need us? Is
this truly part of God's plan for Creation? Doesn't it
plummet us right back into the ego-centred, planet-
centred universe that Copernicus and Bruno and Galileo
overturned?

Well, no, not necessarily. But it does bring up old
questions I haven't thought about since college: When a

tree falls in the forest, if nobody is there to hear it, does it make a sound?

Of course it makes a sound, I said. The tree falls, and sound waves are made, whether they are heard or not. But according to the new physics the sound waves have to be realized by being heard.

In the survey of philosophy I took freshman year, we read some of Bishop Berkeley, and his theory that the stairs outside his study weren't there if he didn't know that they were there. Things have to be apprehended in order to *be*.

During the years when I was writing and not getting published I had the feeling that a book could not be born until it was read and responded to. The reader has to create along with the writer if the book is to come to life.

And what about we, ourselves? I have seen myself growing and changing and developing as my husband and children drew me out of my shell and into being. Surely forty years with Hugh have changed me beyond recognition from the shy, gawky girl he married. Surely his death is going to push me into further growing, further understanding.

If we are responsible for the *being* of things, if we are, as this new theory implies, co-creators with God, this gives the sentient, questioning human being an enormous responsibility. Rather than swelling our egos, it should awaken in us an awed sense of vocation. We human creatures are called to be the eyes and ears and nose and mouth and fingers of this planet. We are called to observe all that is around us, to contemplate it, and to make it real.

Martin Buber expresses it this way:

The world is not something which must be overcome. It is created reality, but reality created to be hallowed.

Everything created has a need to be hallowed and is capable of receiving it: all created corporeality, all created urges and elemental forces of the body. Hallowing enables the body to fulfill the meaning for which it was created.

Hallowing means being made whole and holy by the grace of the Holy Spirit, not by our own effort. It is heaven's gift. So our observing and contemplating needs to be hallowed, or we will fail in that for which we have been called.

This hallowing enables us to have a sense of our planet's place in the universe, to understand that it is part of a magnificent whole, part of the microscopic world of subatomic particles, part of the macrocosmic world of galaxies, and that everything in Creation affects the whole. If we are willing to contemplate all that is around us, to love it, to help make it real, we are adding to the health and beauty and reality of the entire universe.

But we live in a society which seems less and less concerned with reality. True and enduring love is replaced by multiple marriages or the shallow pursuit of physical pleasure. Our standards fall. And as I think of the word *standards* I think of a knight on his horse, holding aloft his standard.

Probably the worst thing that has happened to our understanding of reality has been our acceptance of ourselves as consumers. Our greed is consuming the planet, so that we may quite easily kill this beautiful earth by daily pollution without ever having nuclear warfare. Sex without love consumes, making another person an *object*, not a *subject*. Can we change our vocabulary and our thinking? To do so may well be a matter of life and death. Consumers do not understand that we must live not by

greed and self-indulgence but by observing and contemplating the wonder of God's universe as it is con-
tinually being revealed to us.

Joseph and his brothers lived in a small universe.
There was no church establishment, no educational establishment, no scientific establishment. Establishments, by
their very nature, resist change. The Church resisted the
change from the ego-centred view of the universe, and I
am not sure that our broken Christendom has yet come to
terms with this. Nor has the educational establishment of
today come to terms with the fact that it is currently
inadequate, and that we are becoming a vocabulary-
deprived nation. The scientific establishment only a few
years ago drew back in shock and resistance to the idea of
plate tectonics and continental drift, which seems so ob-
vious now.

But Joseph and his brothers had no such institutions
to grapple with. Their God was with them, and they were
with God, although there is little mention of God or what
they thought of the Creator in the early chapters of
Joseph's story.

Did Simeon and Levi have any compunction about
their slaughter of Shechem and his people? Did it worry
them that they were murderers? Did they care about what
God thought of what they had done? We don't know. We
are not told. We do know that when Jacob, on his
deathbed, gave out his blessings to his sons, Simeon and
Levi were condemned. Actions have consequences.

Jacob's words to them were: *Simeon and Levi are
brethren; instruments of cruelty are in their habitations. . . .
Cursed be their anger, for it was fierce; and their wrath, for it
was cruel. . . . I will scatter them in Israel.*

Harsh words from Jacob. But they were fulfilled; the
tribes of both Simeon and Levi were scattered. We don't

even know what happened to the tribe of Simeon. And the Levites became not a tribe but a priestly clan.

Dinah, the only female in the family, is not included in Jacob's deathbed blessing.

How did Dinah feel about all this, Dinah who had not been a woman for long when she met Shechem?

✳ ✳ ✳

Dinah

Blessed art thou, O Lord our God, King of the universe, who hast not made me a woman.

Oh, yes, that is their favourite benediction, my father and my twelve brothers. You can guess how that makes me feel, the one girl child. After she had me, my mother didn't have any more children. She had, after all, given my father six sons. So there I was, the youngest for a while, the eleventh child for my father, the seventh for my mother, but I was anything but special in her eyes. Or anybody's.

It wasn't that I had an unhappy childhood. We lived with my Grandfather Laban, my mother's and Aunt Rachel's father. We were well fed and cared for, and the older brothers played with me, especially Reuben, and made me feel that they were fond of me, even if my father and his wives and concubines had little use for a girl in their male-oriented world. And then Joseph was born, and then Benjamin, and I wasn't the baby anymore.

By the time Benjamin was born I hadn't been a baby for a long time. I had given myself to a man and seen him and his father and all the people of their tribe murdered in front of my eyes, by two of my brothers, my real brothers, my own mother's sons. They were defending

72

my honour, they said. They didn't want me treated like a whore, they said. Did anybody ask me how I felt, or if I had been treated like a whore? Did anybody ask me whether I wanted to marry Shechem (Oh, my beautiful Shechem)? No. Nobody asked me. They cut him down and I flung myself on his bleeding body, and I don't think they even noticed me, they were so busy slaughtering everybody else.

The ground shrieks with his blood. If they were, as they say, obeying the will of their God, I want no part of that God.

Blessed art thou, O Lord our God, King of the universe who hast not made me a woman.

They can have their god, their bloody god. Bloody as far back as I can remember. I think of my grandfather, Isaac. His father was willing to sacrifice his only child, his son, in a holocaust on Mount Moriah. Even if there was a reprieve at the last minute, a ram to be substituted in Isaac's place, what kind of an erratic and unreasonable god would have made such a demand in the first place? Bloody. Greedy. Only a man would order or carry out that kind of sacrifice.

Where can I turn?

I am lonely. Lonely on earth. In heaven.

How can I turn to my father's and brothers' god?

As for my father, he was still terrified, twenty years after he had foxed him, of Uncle Esau. We were leaving Grandfather Laban's, to go who knows where, nobody told me. Father separated us into two groups so that if Uncle Esau should attack us—if he should, after all these years, still want vengeance—at least half of us might escape. And he, my father, stood alone near the river Jabbok, and someone—God, he said—jumped on him and started wrestling with him. Why? They wrestled, the two of them, all night, and neither one won over the other. If it had really been God, wouldn't God have won?

Anyhow, whoever he was, he gave in to my father's insistence that he be blessed, and for this blessing wounded him on the thigh. My father limps from it still, and will always limp.

Why did this God-creature attack my father, and ask him, "What is your name?" It makes no sense.

They fought all night and nobody won and my father was still terrified of his brother. Why be afraid of Uncle Esau, funny-looking, and hairy, but kind? I didn't meet my uncle until he came to Grandfather Isaac's deathbed. Grandfather Isaac was my father's father, and I never really knew him, not the way I knew Grandfather Laban, with whom I grew up. We all grew up with Grandfather Laban, except Benjamin, who was born on the road between grandfather and grandfather. A bloody road, with my Aunt Rachel bleeding to death after the baby's birth. We could not stop the blood. The ground was red.

I was not close to my Aunt Rachel, though I took after her in looks, rather than my mother. I had my mother's long eyelashes, but I had my Aunt Rachel's beauty, and more, because I was younger. She did not care for me. But it was still a terrible thing to watch the blood gush from her.

I took the baby, tiny, scrawny, red. One of our slave girls was nearly ready to wean her son, and she took Benjamin to nurse. But I rocked him and sang to him, wanting to and not being able to give him for love what she could give for duty.

If only Shechem's seed had flowered within me. Would my brothers have tried to kill that child, too?

He was gentle with me, Shechem, far gentler than my brothers, the gentlest man I'd ever met. The customs of his tribe were different from ours. He wanted to marry me. I would have married him and taken his god for mine, though he and all his tribe were dead before I ever found out about Shechem's god, dead because my brothers said that Shechem could have me for his wife only if he and his father and all the men of his tribe would agree to be circumcised, as my father's and brothers' god requires.

More bloodiness. But Shechem wanted me that much. And so it was done, and while Shechem and the other men were sore and weak my brothers slaughtered them before my eyes.

My father was not pleased.

Oh, no, he was not concerned for me, grieving, weeping my anguish. He was concerned for his own reputation. He said my brothers' murdering ways would make him stink. And we had to leave that place, take up our tents and move. My father's god told him to go to Beth-el, that strange place of his dream of angels. Too many dreams my father had; now Joseph is dreaming, too.

I had dreams, but no one cared.

I would not move from Shechem's body.

Simeon and Levi came to me, those murderers, and I screamed and spat and scratched until they left me alone.

Reuben, the kindest of all my brothers, came quietly and lifted me in his arms and took me away. My mother and Aunt Rachel (who would die so soon) and the concubines washed Shechem's blood from me. It was all that I had of him. Oh, I would that his seed had flowered, would that it had flowered . . .

We journeyed, and Rachel's old nurse died along the way, and then Rachel, and at last we came to Hebron, and I saw my grandfather Isaac, old and dying; and Esau, Uncle Esau, came to help my father bury him.

Uncle Esau was red of hair, on his head, his beard, his body. He wept as he greeted my father and my brothers, and then he came to me and touched my cheek and said, "Do not be sad. He was full of days, my father. It is time for him to be gathered to his people."

How could I be sad for this grandfather I had never known?

Why should I weep for the death of an old man who has lived a life full of years? I weep for Shechem. I weep for the children we will never have (and I would they had been girls). I weep for myself and for my lost life because now, my brothers say, no man will ever want me. Very well. I want no man, not with their bloody gods.

Where are Shechem's gods? If I knew who they were I would turn to them, and perhaps find more gentleness. Were they—are they—gods of war, gods of anger? I think they could not have been, or perhaps they would have protected Shechem and his people.

I would rather have a helpless god than a bloody one.

Unknown gods, I call on you. I do not ask you to do anything to change that which has been done. It has been done.

But would you love me, please? Would you love me?

Judah

thou art he whom thy brethren shall praise: thy hand shall be in the neck of thine enemies; thy father's children shall bow down before thee.

Judah is a lion's whelp: from the prey, my son, thou art gone up: he stooped down, he crouched as a lion, and as an old lion; who shall rouse him up?

The sceptre shall not depart from Judah, nor a lawgiver from between his feet, until Shiloh come; and unto him shall the obedience of the people be.

Binding his foal unto the vine, and his ass's colt unto the choice vine; he washed his garments in wine, and his clothes in the blood of grapes.

His eyes shall be red with wine, and his teeth white with milk.

Genesis 49:8-12

Judah

4

IN THE END, Judah came out pretty well. His name was even given to Jesus—the "lion of Judah." But before that he proved himself to be as complex and flawed as all the major scriptural characters.

Judah, for pragmatic reasons, stopped his brothers from killing Joseph, but was perfectly willing to sell him into Egypt. Joseph, betrayed by his brothers, by his own flesh and blood—Joseph, the spoiled, pampered boy, moved from being a boy to a man on the journey down to Egypt—what "culture shock" for the young Hebrew! The Egyptians were dark of skin, they were not nomads, and they spoke an unfamiliar language.

The Ishmaelites sold Joseph to Potiphar, who was an officer of the ruling Pharaoh of Egypt, and captain of the guard. He was an important man who would be careful of what—or who—he bought. But Joseph, sold and then resold, must have felt like a mere marketplace commodity, sold as casually as an animal is sold. This dehumanization has been the fate of slaves throughout the centuries.

About that time, Scripture says, *Judah left his brothers and went south and pitched his tent in company with an Adullamite named Hirah. There he saw Bathshua the daughter of a Canaanite and married her.*

And now follows a story which, like the story of Dinah, many people have found convenient to forget because it reminds us of our human fallibility. But because it is there, part of Scripture, we are unwise to ignore it, troublesome though it may be.

Judah, Leah's fourth son, is to become important in Hebrew history. When Jacob blesses his sons it is Judah whom he appoints as ruler and progenitor of a royal line rather than the first-born son, Reuben. In the New Testament in the seventh chapter of Hebrews, the fourteenth verse reads: *For it is evident that our Lord sprang out of Judah.*

In the 78th psalm we read, "*He rejected the tent of Joseph and did not choose the tribe of Ephraim. He chose instead the tribe of Judah, and Mount Zion, which he loved.*" And in the seventh chapter of John's Revelation we read, *From all the tribes of Israel there were a hundred and forty-four thousand: twelve thousand from the tribe of Judah*, the tribe of Judah being the first mentioned. And *Judaism* is known as the religion of the Jewish people who, according to my research, believe in one eternal, asexual, caring God.

Why Judah and not Reuben, the first-born? Was it only because Reuben had broken the ancient taboo that he lost his place as head of the family, the first-born? What was so special about Judah?

The first story about Judah is a strange one for a man who is to become as important as this fourth son of Jacob.

Judah married Shuah, as she was called, and went in to her. So she conceived and bore a son, and called his name Er. She conceived again and bore a son, and she called his name Onan. And she conceived again and bore a son, and called his name Shelah.

Judah, according to the custom, took a wife for his first son, Er, a young woman called Tamar. And then what happens? *Er, Judah's firstborn, was wicked in the sight of the Lord, and the Lord slew him.*

Despite the bloody god Dinah's brothers had shown her, the true God of Scripture never killed casually, or without reason. What do you suppose Er did that was so terrible that the Maker of the Universe had to wipe him out? We are not told. Nor are we told whether or not Tamar loved her husband, Er.

In scriptural times it was the custom that when a man died, childless, the brother should then marry the widow and have children by her for his dead brother. This was the custom (known as "levirate marriage") that was referred to when the Sadducees were trying to trap Jesus, and he was asked about the man who had died without issue, and whose six brothers, one after the other, had married the widow, and all died without issue. Who, in heaven, asked the Sadducees, would her husband be?

They were missing the point, Jesus said. For the Sadducees did not believe in the Resurrection at the coming of the Messiah, as did the Pharisees, and as did Martha of Bethany when she said of her dead brother, "I know that he shall rise again at the resurrection at the last day."

So, when Er died, Judah told his second son, Onan, to marry Tamar and beget children for his brother. But Onan knew that the children would not really belong to him, and he was jealous that his seed would belong to his dead brother, so when he went in to Tamar he spilled his seed on the ground, *lest he should give seed to his brother*. And the Lord considered this a travesty of marriage, and destroyed Onan as well as Er. At least we know *why* Onan displeased the Lord—onanism, it is called—"the spilling of the seed." The names of many sexual deviations ("sodomy" is another) come from someone or someplace in Scripture, though sometimes the words have changed their meanings through history. But the seed, as it were, arose in the Old Testament.

Judah told Tamar to return to her father's house and to remain a widow there until Shelah, his youngest son, was an adult old enough to marry her. So Tamar did as Judah bade her and went to her father's house to wait for Shelah to be grown. And waited. And waited.

Time passed, and Judah's wife died, and after he had finished mourning Judah went up with his friend Hirah to check on his sheep shearers. And Tamar was told, *"Your father-in-law is going to Timnath to shear his sheep."* Although Shelah was grown, Judah had not given him Tamar to be his wife. Was it that he was afraid that God was going to kill anyone who married Tamar?

But Tamar knew that the time was overdue for Shelah to marry her. She took off her widow's clothes, put on a veil to cover her face and, according to some translations, perfumed herself and dressed like a prostitute, then sat at a fork in the road on the way to Timnath. Some of the prostitutes at that time and place were temple prostitutes, an integral part of local fertility cults. In any case, Judah saw Tamar, took her for a harlot, and asked her to lie with him, having, of course, no idea that she was his daughter-in-law. And she asked him what he would pay her for her services. He told her, *"I'll give you a kid from my flock."*

"Will you give me a pledge until you send me the kid?" she requested.

"What pledge shall I give you?" he asked.

And she asked him for his signet ring, and his bracelets, and the staff that was in his hand.

When he had given them to her he lay with her, and she conceived by him.

Harlotry. The oldest profession. Prostitutes, while accepted, were considered an underclass, because they took money for what should be given for love. However, when Dinah's brothers complained that Dinah had been treated as a harlot by Shechem, they were talking about a violation of the proprieties, not about selling their sister's body.

Judah hadn't kept his promise to Tamar when Shelah was grown. Therefore, to Tamar, anything she did to get children for Er was justified.

There is a lot to be wondered about here. Had Tamar loved Er so deeply, that she was willing to go to such lengths to get children for him? Did she feel that Er had been stricken down unjustly? Was she angry at God as well as Judah? Not much is told us in these early Scriptures about the feelings of the women. I wonder if Tamar and Dinah ever met and talked about the men they loved, both cut down young and seemingly without good reason.

In those days an unmarried or childless woman was stigmatized. Shelah would have been remedy for both of these problems. So Tamar went away and put back on her widow's clothes.

Judah kept his promise and sent a kid by his friend, Hirah, who had gone with him to the sheep shearing. But

Hirah's search was fruitless. He asked, *"Where is the prostitute who sat here?"*

And he was told, *"There was no prostitute in this place."* And so he had to tell Judah that he had not found the prostitute.

About three months later Judah was told, *"Your daughter-in-law Tamar has played the harlot, and she is pregnant."*

Judah, adhering to the law, asked that Tamar be brought to him and be punished by being burned to death.

But when she was brought to her father-in-law she said, *"The father of my child is the one whose ring and bracelets and staff these are."*

When he saw them, Judah recognized what she showed him, acknowledged them, and admitted, *"She is more in the right than I am, because I did not give Shelah, my son, to her."*

The primitive thinking of a primitive people, perhaps. But it does show that Judah was willing to admit a fault.

And he did not sleep with her again, but as a result of their earlier liaison Tamar had twins in her womb. *As she was giving birth, one infant put out his hand, and the midwife tied a scarlet thread around it, saying, "This one came out first."*

But in fact it was the other baby who was the firstborn, so he was called Perez, which means *breaking out*; the other baby's name was Zerah, which means *redness*, because of the scarlet cord, or, according to another source it can mean *east*, or *brightness*. Was Perez the first breech birth? From him came the Perezite branch of the tribe of Judah; David was a Perezite, and since Tamar is reckoned to be the ancestor of King David (as in the genealogy in 1 Chronicles and in the story of Ruth, as well as in the genealogy at the beginning of Matthew), she is also considered to be the ancestor of Jesus.

What a strange story, interpolated between the selling of Joseph into Egypt, and his early years there. And yet there are no stories in Scripture that do not have a purpose, a proper place. The story of Judah and Tamar tells us something of the customs of the time when the twelve sons of Jacob lived, and something of Judah. Human, as all scriptural characters are human, he was also pragmatic. He was the one who felt that killing Joseph wouldn't accomplish anything. He didn't want blood on his hands, not from any particular compassion for the boy, but because it was not expedient. Better to sell Joseph and at least get some money from the transaction.

When Tamar was accused of harlotry, Judah immediately accepted the customary penalty; she was to be killed; burned, in those days; stoned, later on at the time that Mary was pregnant with Jesus. An odd contradiction, since prostitution was an accepted practise; you just avoided getting caught.

But when Judah discovered that he was the father of Tamar's child, he immediately accepted the responsibility. Yes, he had been tempted by the beauty of the prostitute, and if she was pretending to be a temple prostitute, Tamar represented a religion which was disapproved of by the Hebrews and which they wanted to wipe out. Judah did not try to deny what he had done. Granted, the evidence was laid out before him, his ring and bracelets and staff, but he did not try to rationalize or excuse himself, but said immediately that he was more to blame than Tamar, because he had not given Shelah to her to be her husband.

The judgments of what we consider ordinary morality simply do not work when they are applied to the characters of Scripture. In *A Mixture of Frailties* Robertson Davies writes,

> Moral judgments belong to God, and it is part of God's mercy that we do not have to undertake that heavy part of his work, even when the judgment concerns ourselves.

And what happened to Tamar and Shelah? That we are not told. Did they eventually marry? Did she have a full life as woman, wife, mother?

And what, again, about Er? What about Tamar's grief for the loss of a husband? How long had they been married before Er was struck down? Not very long, it would seem. Certainly nowhere near the forty years I was married to Hugh, so that my life with him has been far longer than my life before our marriage. But what a shocking grief for Tamar to have her husband wiped out by God!

Our God is a consuming fire, we read. *God is like a refiner's fire*. Moses saw God in a burning bush, a bush which burned and yet was not consumed. We are to be refined in the fire like silver. Shadrach, Meshach, and Abednego walked through the flames. Jesus promised a baptism "with the Spirit and with fire." The Spirit descended and descends in tongues of fire.

Satan has tried to take fire over as his own image, teasing, tormenting us with the idea of the flames of hell. Dante understood the wrongness of the metaphor; in his *Inferno*, the most terrible circle of fire is *cold*. The purifying fire comes not from Satan, but from God.

T.S. Eliot writes of the Holy Spirit,

> The dove descending breaks the air
> With flame of incandescent terror . . .

Who then devised the torment? Love.
Love is the unfamiliar Name
Behind the hands that wove
The intolerable shirt of flame
Which human power cannot remove.
We only live, only suspire
Consumed by either fire or fire.

The purifying fire of God, or the deadly cold fire of
Satan. Tamar, a woman of great courage, went through
the fire of suffering. I wish we had been told more of her
story.

But through Tamar the genealogy of David is traced,
and then, Jesus.

And here is an interesting thing: Jesus's genealogy is
traced through his *adoptive* father, Joseph, who was of the
tribe of David, emphasizing that to the Hebrew an
adopted child is a real child and part of the blood line.

The earlier Joseph, having been sold into Egypt, knew
nothing of all this.

✳ ✳ ✳

Judah

Blessed art thou, O Lord our God, King of the universe,
who hast not made me a woman.

Trouble. That's all that women have brought us.
Trouble. My mother was not loved by my father, though
she gave him six sons. It was our Aunt Rachel he loved,
and that brought trouble to us all. Rachel, so sure of
herself and her beauty. So sure that she was loved. Is still
loved, for she still troubles my father's heart, so that he
cannot see straight, not even as straight as my mother. He

has eyes only for Joseph, who lords it over us all from his pedestal of favouritism.

Enough of Joseph. May we never again hear from Joseph. May we never again hear of Joseph.

My wife. She was my wife, but she brought me nothing but trouble. My sons, the children of my loins, are dead because of a woman. Tamar. Beautiful. Oh, yes, though while Shuah was alive she saw to it that I noticed nobody but Shuah. But Tamar was death to my sons. How could I give her Shelah, when she had killed Er and Onan?

And then she tricked me, dressing like a temple prostitute, serving alien gods—gods who are women, tricksters, with their moon playing tricks on our hearts, so that I fell for the tricksters' wiles.

It is taboo to lie with your son's wife, but because I was tricked into it God was not displeased with me, nor with these two new sons.

Blessed art thou, O Lord our God, King of the Universe. I do not understand your ways. I am only grateful that you accept me as I am, without tricks, and bless me with two young sons.

Dan

shall judge his people, as one of the tribes of Israel.

Dan shall be a serpent by the way, an adder in the path, that biteth the horse heels, so that his rider shall fall backward.

Genesis 49:16-17

Dan
5

WE DON'T KNOW MUCH ABOUT DAN, except that he was Jacob's fifth son, Bilhah's first child, and that he was the head of the tribe of Dan, one of the twelve tribes of Israel. He conspired with his brothers to sell Joseph into Egypt. Dan was blessed by his father, and blessed by Moses, and his children took in battle a place called Laish, *a people that were quiet and secure, and they smote them with the edge of the sword and burned the city with fire.* Once again land was simply taken from the people who lived there. *And they called the name of the city Dan, after Dan, their father.*

Then, as we read on, in *Judges*, they set up a graven image (though of what, we do not know), and in doing that, alas, they were not unusual.

In Joseph's eyes Egypt must have been full of graven images, for the Pharaohs, with the exception of Ikhnaton, worshipped a pantheon of gods, and the temples were painted with their likenesses, and sphinxes and lions and elephants were carved to line the avenues of temples and palaces.

Not only were there strange gods in Egypt, but strange people, darker in color than Joseph, and speaking a strange language. In their knowledge of astronomy, they were far more sophisticated than the nomadic Hebrews. And Joseph was sold to a man who lived in a palace, and not a tent. He was extraordinarily adaptable, Joseph, toughened by the rough trip into Egypt, where he was sold to Potiphar, who was in the service of the Pharaoh.

Joseph had the perceptiveness to look around him, to observe and contemplate all that he saw.

If we human beings are called to be observers and contemplators, this calling is given reality because it is God's gift to us (as it was to Joseph), and this is what hallows it. It is nothing we can take pride in. At the end of this twentieth century since the birth of Jesus we cannot return to the old arrogance of considering ourselves to be the only focus of God's interest. We are called to observe the wonders of creation, to contemplate them, and then to make an appropriate response.

Our understanding of the stars in their courses and our own little planet has changed and expanded enormously since Copernicus and Galileo and Newton and Einstein and Hawking. And it will go right on changing; we must rejoice in it, rather than turning our backs in fear. Perhaps on his long journey south, Joseph also learned to move without fear from one way of looking at creation to a far different way, to let his images move and expand with his knowledge. We must learn that same openness.

The discoveries made since the heart of the atom was opened have irrevocably changed our view of the universe and creation. Our great radio telescopes are picking up echoes of that primal act of creation which expanded to become all the stars in their courses. It would seem that the beginning of all things came from something so incredibly tiny as to be nothing, a sub-sub-atomic particle so infinitesimal that it is difficult even to imagine. So science brings us back to a God who created *ex nihilo*. And who then took that early primordial soup, that chaos, and made from it night and day and galaxies and solar systems and all creatures great and small.

There are many theories today which I find immensely exciting theologically, but I want to sit lightly enough to it all so that if something new and perhaps contradictory is revealed I won't be thrown off-center, as were Darwin's frightened opponents, but will go on being excited about the marvelousness of being—of snowflake and starfish and geranium and galaxy. There is nothing too small or unimportant (and surely when he was sold into Egypt, Joseph was small and unimportant) to make a difference.

Much of what I read in the way of quantum mechanics and particle physics and the new theories of chaos and topology and fractals is over my head. Never mind. The fact that they are difficult doesn't stop me from continuing to grapple with new ideas, because *all* ideas ultimately come from God who made it all. There's a fascinating and as yet still unexplained little mathematical problem noticed first by Paul Dirac (and there's a joke about Dirac: "There is no god, and Dirac is his prophet"): numbers with the order of magnitude of one followed by forty zeros keep appearing, to everybody's surprise. For instance, the ratio of the huge electromagnetic force between two particles to the much weaker gravitational force between them is one, followed by forty zeroes. The number that would equal the mass of the universe is one followed by forty zeroes multiplied by itself. The present temperature of space requires the expansion rate at the birth of the universe to be one followed by forty zeroes. Now, that is all certainly above my non-mathematical head, but it still intrigues me.

Why forty? At this point nobody seems to have any idea. I have never before thought of forty as being a number of any particular significance. But wait. After Noah boarded the ark it rained for forty days and forty nights. Moses and the Hebrew children took forty years to cross the desert to the Promised Land. Moses on Mt. Sinai talked with God for forty days. Elijah was fed for forty days by a big, black bird. Jesus, after his baptism, fasted for forty days. And after the Resurrection he stayed with his friends for forty days before the Ascension. Paul, evidently impressed by the potency of forty, said that he had received forty stripes but one.

And in Pharaonic Egypt, the period of mourning was forty days. In the Middle Ages in Europe someone seeking sanctuary was protected for forty days.

And I was married for forty years.

A potent number. One day we may understand why it is turning up so frequently in the mathematics of the universe, unless we try to hang onto our present state of knowledge as the church tried to hang onto the old theory of planet earth as the center of the universe.

It was pointed out to me by a young astrophysicist friend that gravity, too, plays a significant part in planetary life. Our gravity is at exactly the fine-tuned strength that will permit the evolution of planets which are capable of supporting life. If gravity were a fraction weaker, all stars would be red dwarfs; if it were a fraction stronger, all stars would be blue giants; and suns like ours, strong young suns with planetary systems, would not be possible, and there would be no sentient life what-soever.

Does this seem to be in conflict with creationism? Why? If God is omnipotent and all powerful, can't the Creator create in any way that Love chooses, and so expand our metaphor? The important thing is that the universe was made by Love, and belongs to Love.

My astrophysicist friend showed me some complex scientific charts which he was taking with him to Amsterdam, where he was in charge of a planetology conference. At the bottom of one of these charts, black with equations like $c = 2.998 \times 10^{10}$ cm s-1 (and that's one of the simpler ones) he had typed out, "He showed me a little thing, the quantity of an hazelnut, in the palm of my hand; and it was round as a ball. I looked thereupon with the eye of my understanding, and thought: what may this be? And was answered generally thus: It is all that is made."

It is a great comfort to me to find a highly respected astrophysicist quoting Lady Julian of Norwich in a series of scientific diagrams to be presented to other scientists.

Sometimes it is the acuteness of pain or anxiety that heightens our awareness of God's creation. Not long before Hugh died I went on a walk with two young friends who were planning their wedding, and who were deeply affected by Hugh's illness. One of them picked up a tiny blue eggshell, recently vacated by a fledgling. And for us there in the little shell was all of creation. A hazelnut. A robin's egg. The Milky Way.

Paul Dirac believes that all of the seeming coincidences in the makeup of the universe reveal a deep connection between microcosm and macrocosm, between astrophysics and particle physics. And physicists are actually asking, "May it be that life is of real importance to the universe?" John Wheeler takes an extreme anthropic view, feeling that we human beings are *needed* by the universe, that there has to be "observer participation" in order for the universe to be sustained.

Are we as important as that? It could be a pretty ego-swelling thought, plunging us back into the smugness of the old sandwich theory, with the universe totally earth-centered. Or is the anthropic theory, instead, ego-shattering? What have we human beings done with our participation in the great work of Creation? Are we being co-creators with God? Or are we being destroyers—consumers? Can a consumer co-create? Are we honouring God's Creation, when our greed causes us to pollute our planet?

And here is an extraordinary thing: among some right-wing, fundamentalist Christians it is seen as a sign of atheism or communism to care about the ecology of the planet God has given us to live on. I find that difficult to comprehend. How can Christians view stewardship of what God called good, very good, as being unChristian?

A longing for peace, too, is seen as atheist or communist. God help us! I have lived in a century of war, and I long for peace. The psalmist cries out, "*My soul hath long dwelt with him that hateth peace. I am for peace; but when I speak, they are for war.*"

"*Peace I leave with you,*" Jesus said. "*My peace I give unto you.*"

How can we reject that peace?

Perhaps those who view as atheist or communistic a concern for the planet or a longing for peace are also unable to see God's creation as greater than we expected. In a book on particle physics the writer, a physicist, remarked that the universe seems to be far more "imaginary" than formerly had been believed.

Which leads to the question: Whose imagination?

If it is the scientists', if it is our human imaginations alone, then I don't think I trust it. But if it is God's, if *everything that is* is held in the mind of God, then our "observer participation" makes considerable sense. There are hints all through Scripture that God calls us to work with El on the great story of Creation, because the Maker of the story is constantly coming in and being part of it, helping us along in the great drama, and going to such lengths to be part of the story that the Power that created the universe willingly limited Elself to the form of a tiny baby.

The Word: the Word that loved us so much that it enfleshed itself for us at Christmas, hallowing our humanness, strengthening us to be what we are called to be.

Christmas fills me with utter awe. The incredible sacrifice of all Power and Glory in coming to be part of the human endeavor leaves me breathless. How can we have trivialized this amazing action of love by letting the media turn us into consumers! Christmas should be greeted with the silence of awe and wonder, as the great and mighty Word leaped into the womb of a human girl, and was born as all of us are born.

In my Goody Book I've copied out these unattributed words:

"Trumpets! Lightnings! The earth trembles! but into the Virgin's womb thou didst descend with noiseless tread."

And, again, "No longer do the Magi bring presents to Fire and Sun, for this child made Sun and Fire."

This is a story so wildly incredible that the world has tried to tame it, but it cannot be tamed, and we, like the Magi, are called to observe, contemplate, stand there, bring our gifts, and offer them. At our best, our offerings make us more human. At our worst, they make us less human. When religion causes judgmentalism, suspicion, and hate, there is something wrong with religion. It has become dehumanizing, and therefore it is bad religion, and we become once more a horror and a hissing and an everlasting reproach.

War dehumanizes. Hate, fear, revenge dehumanize. There has been too much dehumanization in this century. Two thousand years ago Jesus came and called people to become more human, to pull us back to the Image in which we were created. And that is still our calling.

It is our very humanness which enables us to observe and contemplate and, ultimately, to hallow or to affirm holiness. The more human we are, the better we are able to understand who is doing the calling. It is not an abstract principle of creation. It bears no resemblance to that "humanism" which puts man back in the center and has no need for God. Were not Adam and Eve called to observe and contemplate? Yet after they ate the forbidden fruit, they became self-conscious, thinking only of their nakedness rather than the loveliness around them.

Why did it matter to them that they were naked? Why didn't they look at their beautiful created bodies with joy? What caused them to feel shame? Shame was not an appropriate response. How did the tempter manage to stir up guilt feelings? Guilt for their nakedness, rather than for dishonouring their Maker's request. It was false guilt, certainly, blinding them to the real. What God made was perfect and to be rejoiced in. Was their shame the beginning of all our sexual confusions and repressions and lusts?

When they stopped responding to God's calling them to observe and contemplate all that had been created, they could no longer hallow.

To observe and contemplate what God has made is an act of joy. The moment Adam and Eve felt shame they lost the joy. Where there is no joy the presence of God is obscured.

Thomas Traherne writes,

You never enjoy the world aright, till the sea itself floweth in your veins, till you are clothed with the heavens, and crowned with the stars; and perceive yourself to be the sole heir of the whole world, and more so, because men [male and female] are in it who are every one sole heirs as well as you. Till you can sing and rejoice and delight in God, and in good as coming from God . . . you never enjoy the world.

This is a perfect description of how we human creatures are called to observe and contemplate. To enjoy thus is to shout, "This is holy!" To enjoy thus is to be enjoyed by God!

It seems odd that those who take the anthropic view seem not to have noticed that we have made a mess of it, with our lack of joy, our overblown sense of self-importance. How could human creatures who have truly observed and contemplated a child, any child, then blast that child with napalm? How could anyone who has ever loved anybody plant a bomb in a plane and wantonly kill several hundred people? How could human creatures who have truly observed the beauty of the planet, who have enjoyed the world aright then proceed to foul it with greed and stupidity and pollution? with the ugliness of inner cities which surely bear no resemblance to the Celestial City? with strip mining and deforestation and smoke belching from factory chimneys—and how much of the increase in cancer comes from polluted food and air and water?

How did we get a Pentagon and a stock market and state mental institutions? (When I was a child there was no Pentagon.) Have we people of this planet gone mad?

But it is not too late. We are given a second chance, a whole series of second chances. God is indeed merciful. It is not too late to mend the terrible damage we have done—not single-handedly, but simply in our own lives, in our own living and in our dying. We have cleaned up the dying Hudson River and a dead Great Lake. If we will, we can.

What have the advances in technocracy done to our humanness? I am all for technology when it is used with wisdom. It is technology which enabled the eye surgeon to give me sight. But it is technocracy that dehumanizes.

There has been more change in this century than in all the preceding centuries put together. It is difficult to be observers and contemplators in the face of constant movement, of shift and flux. On the news not long ago I heard that a third of our purchases in the next decade will be objects which have not yet been invented. This produces uncertainty, and uncertainty produces fear, and fear produces rage. Young school-age friends of mine in New York have been beaten up, more than once, by other boys—not for money, just for anger, as racial unrest grows.

The last Christmas Hugh and I had together I wrote
this poem for our Christmas letter:

> Observe and contemplate.
> Make real. Bring to be.
> Because we note the falling tree
> The sound is truly heard.
> Look! The sunrise! Wait—
> It needs us to look, to see,
> To hear, and speak the Word.
>
> Observe and contemplate
> The cosmos and our little earth.
> Observing, we affirm the worth
> Of sun and stars and light unfurled.
> So, let us, seeing, celebrate
> The glory of God's incarnate birth
> And sing its joy to all the world.
>
> Observe and contemplate.
> Make real. Affirm. Say Yes,
> And in this season sing and bless
> Wind, ice, snow; rabbit and bird;
> Comet and quark; things small and great.
> Oh, observe and joyfully confess
> The birth of Love's most lovely Word.

We need to take time to step back, to observe, to
contemplate. We need to acknowledge with as much
honesty as Judah that Christianity has been so judgmental and so unloving that it has turned many people away.

Where are our heroes and heroines? What we call "role models" today? How do we stop being a horror and a hissing and an everlasting reproach, and instead become a joy to our Creator and to each other?

John Heuss, in his article, "The True Function of a Christian Church" writes, "It is customary for all of us to lay the blame for public indifference to religion at the door of the secularism and materialism of our age," of our longing for the fleshpots of Egypt. But then he goes on to say that the church is no longer offering a living, loving alternative. "Perhaps our contribution in these days is not so much the evangelizing of the world as it is the Christianizing of the Church itself."

Let us never forget that *Christianizing* starts all the way back at the beginning of Genesis, when Christ, the Word, shouted the galaxies into being. Jesus lived with us for a short lifetime, but Christ is with us always—was, in the beginning, is now, and always will be.

In *Daniel*, when Shadrach, Meshach, and Abednego are in the fiery furnace, King Nebuchadnezzar says, "But I see four men in the furnace! And one of them looks like the son of God!" So there was Christ, in the furnace with the three young men, although Christ was not yet known by that name. God did not take them out of the fiery furnace. God was in there with them.

As God was with Joseph in Egypt.

Immediately after the birth of Tamar's twins we read: *And Joseph was brought down to Egypt, and Potiphar, an officer of Pharaoh, captain of the guard, an Egyptian, bought him from the hands of the Ishmaelites who had brought him there.*

And the Lord was with Joseph, and he was a prosperous man; and he was in the house of his master the Egyptian. And

*his master saw that the Lord was with him, and that the Lord
made all that he did to prosper in his hand.*

*And Joseph found grace in Potiphar's sight, and he served
him, and he made him overseer over his house, and all that he
had he put into his hand.*

*And it came to pass from the time that he had made him
overseer in his house, and over all that he had, that the Lord
blessed the Egyptian's house for Joseph's sake, and the blessing
of the Lord was upon all that he had in the house, and in the
field.*

The Joseph who could successfully manage Potiphar's large estate had certainly matured from the con-
ceited child whose only duty was to go check on his
brothers when they were tending their flocks. He had
learned a great deal.

It must have taken considerable time from the moment when Potiphar bought himself another slave, to the
time when Joseph was put in charge of everything that
Potiphar had: months, perhaps years.

Joseph had to observe and contemplate. For him,
Egypt must have been what is now called "culture
shock." He had grown up as a nomad, with a tent for his
home. Potiphar lived in a stone palace. Potiphar who, as
an Egyptian, probably worshipped many gods, was not
only tolerant of Joseph's God, but saw that this God was
taking care of Joseph. Perhaps he was willing to accept
Joseph's God into his pantheon of gods. We are not told
what Joseph thought, only that God blessed him.

From our small hotel balcony in Cairo Hugh and I
looked down at the modern city, dazzled at the view of
the Nile, and even more dazzled as we looked across the
city to the silhouettes of the pyramids—shadowy tri-
angles in the distance. Below us on the street we heard the

constant honking of horns, from cars caught in a never-ending traffic jam, made worse by an occasional horse or donkey cart moving at its own deliberate pace. The ancient and modern worlds seemed as tangled as the traffic.

There's a great fascination to Egypt, with its rich history, largely known because of its complex religion. When I was a child growing up in New York on 82nd Street, my short cut to the park to play hopscotch or skip rope was through the Metropolitan Museum. This was in a gentler day when museum security could afford to be loose, and it often took me an hour or more to get to the park. My favourite place was the Egyptian wing where I was free to wander through the reconstructed tombs. At that time one of my most reread Bible stories was that of Joseph and his dreams and his experiences in Egypt, and the Egyptian section of the museum made it more real for me.

But seeing Egypt with Hugh was a revelation to my understanding of Scripture. Abraham, Isaac, Jacob, all made trips to Egypt, which was as different from their desert setting as another planet. And yet Egypt was bordered by desert. Wherever the Nile flood waters did not reach was desert. The fertile valley was little more than a narrow strip kept fruitful by the spring flooding of the river.

I am grateful to have the memory of Egypt with Hugh, for what we have had can never be taken away from us. The sand blew in our faces as it must have blown when Joseph was there. The smells, too, took me back many centuries, smells of donkey and camel dung and cooking food and many bodies. Sound is different. The new sounds obscure the old. Horns honking: that will always be Cairo for me. And there is the sound of loud speakers amplifying the recording of the muezzin calling the faithful to prayer. Once upon a time (but long after Joseph) it would have been a real man up in the minaret making the strange and beautiful call. The mechanical voice has lost the resonance of life.

Then there are sounds of cars backfiring and sometimes the sounds of gunshots. Sounds of war, of people divided against each other. Joseph's brothers divided him from the home tents and sold him (and what would have happened if they hadn't?).

But they did, and Joseph learned. He was a handsome young man, and honest, and he honoured his master. Somewhere on the journey between Canaan and Egypt he had developed integrity. He did well. Potiphar trusted him, and Joseph did not betray that trust.

Potiphar's wife, who lusted after him, is one of the nastiest women one could imagine. As soon as she looked at the young Hebrew she wanted him.

In the French Jerusalem Bible Potiphar is referred to as a eunuch, which I find both confusing and suggestive. Why would a woman marry a man who was a eunuch? Historically, eunuchs did not marry. On the other hand, if Potiphar were a eunuch, it would explain, if not excuse, the behavior of Potiphar's wife. It is more likely that Potiphar was an officer of Pharaoh, and an ordinary man, who needed someone in his household he could trust implicitly. And that someone was Joseph.

Potiphar's wife (we are never given her name) would have been well-dressed according to the Egyptian fashion, wearing jewels, and heavy make-up which was as much a protection from the sun as an aid to beauty. The deep black around women's eyes was originally to diffuse the sun's rays, and the red paint on the lips was to protect them from dryness. But they soon became symbols of beauty.

Egyptian men were also dressed ornately, and to an over-sophisticated woman Joseph must have seemed simple and earthy. Potiphar's wife wanted Joseph, and she ordered him bluntly, "Lie with me."

But Joseph refused, telling Potiphar's wife that his master trusted him with everything. *"Nor has he kept anything back from me but you, because you are his wife. How then can I do this great wickedness and sin against God?"*

Potiphar's wife knew nothing about Joseph's God, and his refusal made her want him more than ever, and whenever Potiphar was away she tried to tempt him. *One day when they were alone in the house she caught him by his garment, saying "Lie with me." But he left his garment in her hand and fled and ran outside.*

That gave the scorned woman her chance for revenge. She called all the other servants and told them that her husband had *"brought in a Hebrew to mock us. He came in to me to lie with me, and I cried out with a loud voice. And it happened, when he heard that I lifted my voice and cried out, that he left his garment with me and fled outside."*

She kept Joseph's garment and told the same lie to Potiphar when he came home. *"The Hebrew servant whom you brought to us came in to me to mock me,"* and she told her husband that she had screamed, and that Joseph had run away, leaving his garment with her.

And Potiphar, believing his wife, was outraged, and put Joseph in prison.

Again Joseph was betrayed, this time by a woman who felt herself scorned and had to lash out and see to it that Joseph was punished. She was not a nice woman, Potiphar's wife.

And Joseph lay in prison where he had plenty of time to observe and contemplate.

✳ ✳ ✳

Potiphar's Wife

He is fat, fat and lazy, the old Pot. His belly is as big as though he is pregnant. But he does not produce. He lets others do his work for him. Just as well. They do better than he could.

I was given to him in marriage. Given to a man old enough to be my father, and who was willing to pay a large bride price and to ask little from my parents, who had little to give. I did not expect him to be as greedy for me, for my young body. I had thought that since he was old, our bed would be a quiet place. But his lust was, it seemed, insatiable, as night after night he drove himself into me, hurting me with his violence, and with never a thought for my pleasure or pain. No wonder he was exhausted by day and let others do for him any work he could escape.

I found love, then, with one of the young servants who was gentle with me, concerned for my needs, waking in me undreamed-of pleasure. But he left, moving away from our household, leaving me aroused but, after his leaving, with no way to satisfy my need. And Potiphar grew more and more demanding. I do not know whether or not he suspected the young servant, or whether or not his suspicion caused my lover's departure.

I am beautiful. I could have anyone I wanted, and I sometimes did. But I was no longer satisfied.

Then the young Hebrew came, bought from some wandering Ishmaelites. Oh, he was beautiful, with his curling hair and beard, his lean young body, his dark, exciting eyes. At first he simply did his work, quietly, not speaking, for he did not know our language. Then, as he began to be able to speak, Potiphar gave him more and more responsibility until he was managing first our household, and, at last, the entire estate.

Why, I thought, had Potiphar bought him, if not for me?

So I turned to him, the young Hebrew. I offered myself to him.

And he said *No*. Something about his god and honouring Potiphar or not dishonouring Potiphar or some such nonsense.

He has only one god, so I went to the temple of Isis, of Osiris, and On, to temples whose gods are vultures, or crocodiles, or great, venomous snakes. Surely all our gods can over-ride his one god.

And still he said *No*. I rimmed my eyes with more than the usual kohl, rouged my lips and cheeks and the lobes of my ears, oiled and perfumed my hair.

And all I got for my pains was his garment, and with it I destroyed him. Potiphar has thrown him into jail, and that will be the end of him.

But oh! I wish he had not gone.

Naphtali

is a hind let loose, he giveth goodly words.
Genesis 49:21

Naphtali

6

NAPHTALI WAS BILHAH'S SECOND SON, Jacob's sixth, and we don't know much more about him than we do about Dan. He was the head of the tribe that bore his name, and he shared his territory with the Canaanites. Twice his tribe answered the call of Gideon to battle against invading Midianites.

Jacob blesses this son, but tells him that although he was born a mountain ewe, wild and free, he would give birth to lambs in the fold, a veiled warning that Naphtali's land would lose its independence. Moses, too, blesses him, saying, *"Naphtali, sated with favour, and filled with Yahweh's blessing, possesses the sea and the high lands."* And, in the Song of Deborah, Naphtali is lauded with Zebulun for helping in the bloody battle against Sisera.

Otherwise we know little about him. He went along with most of the other brothers in selling Joseph into Egypt as a slave.

Joseph had done so well in Potiphar's house that again he was specially favoured (much as Jacob had favoured him). Yet once again he was betrayed. It must have been bitter indeed for Joseph to be put in jail by Potiphar because he had refused to betray his master. And perhaps Potiphar did not escape a tug of jealousy; Joseph was younger than he, handsome, and in the full strength of his youth.

What must Joseph have thought about as he lay in prison? There were as yet no Psalms to comfort him, no written Scripture to give him guidance and hope. Again, he was plunged into the darkness of betrayal, alone with his thoughts, in a strange land among strange people. And this time he had been slandered as well as betrayed.

Slander from the mouth of a selfish and greedy woman is more understandable than slander from those who loudly proclaim themselves as Christians. Potiphar's wife slandered because she didn't get her own way. "Christians" often appear to slander for love of slander. "Christian" groups—or individuals—read books *looking for* key words which will enable them to say the book is not Christian, or that it is pornographic.

I have received a good bit of this treatment. When *A Wrinkle in Time* was yet again attacked during Hugh's last summer, at a time when he was at home between hospital stays, he said, "They are afraid," and I suspect that he was right. It is particularly ironic that this book should come under fire since it was the book—my seventh—with which I realized that my work is vocation, not career. My work is God's gift to me, and I try to serve it, and in *Wrinkle* I was writing about that perfect love that casts out fear.

One night when I had received a gratuitous attack on one of my books by a woman concerned with smelling out books she considered unChristian—and her tools for condemnation did not include either reading the book or knowing what it was about—I turned to Scripture for comfort and perspective and opened to the Beatitudes and read, suddenly in a completely new and different way, *"Blessed are you when men shall revile you and persecute you, and shall say all manner of evil against you falsely, for my sake. Rejoice, and be exceeding glad, for great is your reward in heaven; for so persecuted they the prophets which were before you."*

This did not mean that I was thinking of myself as one of the prophets, but that I was reading about the present, rather than about the long past. Holding the Bible in my hands, I knew that I was hoping to turn all my writing towards my Maker, to write for the sake of the Creator, and not for this small servant who struggles with words in order to serve the Word.

Thank God we do not have to make moral judgments, that this is God's prerogative, not ours. Hugh again pointed out that the attackers are afraid, afraid that their safe little God-in-a-box may not be safe at all—loving, perfectly loving, but not safe in a finite sense. Or afraid that their cozy and exclusive beliefs may possibly be too narrow. But when we truly have faith in God's love, then the wideness of God's mercy does not terrify. And Hugh's pointing out the fear of the censors was witness to his own courage in the face of terrible illness.

I would not knowingly or willingly read a blasphemous or pornographic book, though I have found some on the bestseller lists. But such books do not hurt me, because I am safe in God's love. I may be made uncomfortable or unhappy or angry by such a book because it is worthless or ugly, but it is not going to hurt me or shake my faith in the joyous power of love. And maybe it will have lessons to teach me, even if they are only to let me know what *not* to do. But it will not frighten me, because there is no place too dark for Love's light to shine, no place of filth without a spot where Love can come in and clean.

Then I came across these words of Brother Andrew, an Episcopal monk:

> . . . fear can lead us to a compulsion to try to convert others to our point of view. We feel threatened by the possibility of our being wrong. [Oh, yes, I understand this. Hugh warned me of this.] Or we dread the possible changes that might enter our lives if we changed our minds about an important issue.

So I must be very careful not to fear the stinging accusations, but to look at them objectively and compassionately without imposing moral judgments.

I turn to the Psalms not only when I need comfort, but as a daily *devoir*, reading the Psalms each day so that at the end of a month I have read all one hundred and fifty. One evening I was reading in Coverdale's translation, and came to the verses about Joseph's imprisonment, and read, *The iron entered his soul.* In most other translations it reads, *They put an iron collar on his neck.* But I like better the implications of *the iron entered his soul.* Joseph was still in the process of maturing, developing from the pampered boy to the strong man.

We are not told how Joseph felt about the God of Abraham, Isaac, and Jacob while he was in prison. We do not know whether or not he prayed, whether or not he was angry at those who betrayed him and forsook him, whether or not he remembered his dreams of grandeur.

What could have seemed more remote to him as he lay in prison?

But, just as Joseph had done well in the house of Potiphar, so he did well in prison, *for the Lord was with Joseph, and shewed mercy, and gave him favour in the sight of the keeper of the prison. And the keeper of the prison committed to Joseph's hand all the prisoners that were in the prison; and the keeper of the prison no longer had to do anything because the Lord was with Joseph and made everything he did to prosper.*

We are not told of Joseph's own dreams while he was in prison. But when the butler and the baker offended Pharaoh, and he put them in the prison where Joseph was now in charge, we learn about their dreams.

The butcher, the baker, the candlestick maker were all there in jail with Joseph. No television, no radio, no newspapers, nothing to keep them in touch with the outside world except the gossip of the jailer.

But Joseph was a dreamer, and so he must have dreamed. Perhaps by now he had learned to keep his dreams to himself.

Most of us dream, even if we don't remember our dreams. I have several every night, and I don't bother to write them down unless they seem to have special significance, otherwise I wouldn't write anything else. The dreams come in three categories—ordinary, easily translated dreams; dreams that are story, in which I may be only an observer, not a participant, but stories which are enough on their own (only twice have I used a dream in something I was writing); and the special dreams, which are pure gifts of grace.

I had one of the golden dreams shortly before Hugh got ill. It started out grey. I was with a great many people in a wasteland of mud and dirt. We could look through a high hurricane fence into a large sunny garden full of flowers and trees, and brightly dressed people singing and laughing together. But the great gates were closed against us. And someone told me that it was my responsibility to speak to the people with me outside the garden and to warn them of their hardness of heart. And I cried out, "How can I possibly be the one to do that when there is still coldness in my own heart, when I have not yet learned fully to forgive, when I haven't learned nearly enough about love . . . ?"

Then I looked up and the gates were swinging open.

While Hugh was dying my dreams were mostly garbled, neither good nor bad, jumbles of colour and confusion. I was tired, bone weary. I would take out some of my frustration over what was happening to Hugh by taking the whacker and going after the weedy sumac trees which were springing up and obscuring my view of the western hills. Weeds were profuse in the vegetable garden, and I made great piles of them. Almost every evening we ate out of the garden, medleys of green and yellow beans, peas, broccoli, baby beets and carrots, reminding me of the harvest psalms where the hills dance for joy.

What was Joseph given to eat in prison? Nothing like the tender green bounty of our vegetable garden.

How long was he there before the butcher and the baker told him their dreams and things once again changed for him? Not a short time. Months, at the very least. Was he ever afraid? Did he turn to the God of his fathers for courage and strength? We are told that God was with him, but we are not told of his own awareness of God.

While Hugh was dying I was acutely aware of God, far more than when things go on in the ordinary way. Without that awareness how would I have survived? I wondered, as the weeks dragged on, if I was being faithful enough in prayer. I went through the motions, said the words, read the Scripture passages, but I was not always there.

And the wonderful thing is that this is all right. We don't have to be perpetually and flawlessly faithful. Only God is that. In God's love I may be angry, I may be anguished, I may be exhausted, but I am not afraid, because God is love and Love casts out fear.

Perhaps Joseph was closer to God in prison than when he was bragging about his dreams.

And the butler and the baker each dreamed a dream, and the dreams disturbed them. Joseph came in to them in the morning and looked at them, and saw that they were sad. So he asked them, "Why do you look so sad today?"

And they said to him, "We have each dreamed a dream, and there is no interpreter of it."

And Joseph said, "Do not interpretations belong to God? Tell me your dreams."

Joseph had learned that dreams belong to God, and that the interpretation of dreams belongs to God. During the long nights in jail he must have pondered his own grand dreams which seemed far indeed from the possibility of fulfillment. And yet he still believed in them, and that they came from God. But now, rather than having a swelled head, he was increasing in probity and trustworthiness.

The chief butler told his dream to Joseph and said to him, "In my dream I saw a vine set before me, and in the vine were three branches, and it was as though the vine budded, and the blossoms shot forth, and from their clusters came ripe grapes. And Pharaoh's cup was in my hand, and I took the grapes and pressed them into Pharaoh's cup, and I gave the cup into Pharaoh's hand."

And Joseph said to him, "This is the interpretation of it: the three branches are three days, yet within these three days shall Pharaoh lift up your head and restore you into your place, and you shall deliver Pharaoh's cup into his hand, and once again you will be as you were when you were his chief butler. But remember me when it is well with you, and show kindness to me, I beg you, and mention me to Pharaoh, and bring me out of this prison. For indeed I was stolen away out of the land of the Hebrews, and here in Egypt also I have done nothing that they should put me into this dungeon."

When the chief baker saw that the interpretation was good, he said to Joseph, "In my dream, behold I had three white baskets on my head, and in the uppermost basket there was all manner of sweetmeats for Pharaoh, and the birds ate them out of the basket on my head."

And Joseph answered and said, "This is the interpretation of your dream. The three baskets are three days, and within three days Pharaoh will lift up your head from off you, and he will hang you on a tree, and the birds shall eat your flesh."

And it came to pass the third day, which was Pharaoh's birthday, that he made a feast for all his servants, and he lifted up the head of the chief butler and the chief baker among his servants. And he restored the chief butler unto his butlership again, and he gave the cup into Pharaoh's hand. But he hanged the chief baker, as Joseph had interpreted to him. Yet the chief butler did not remember Joseph, but forgot him.

So it goes. Once the chief butler became chief butler again, once things were going well for him, he forgot the man who had predicted this.

And the chief baker was dead, and we do not know why. Were there good reasons? Or was it the arbitrary, irrational whim of a ruler with enormous power? Monarchs do not always behave rationally. Power sometimes causes the powerful to treat other humans as mere objects. But the record doesn't tell us why one man was promoted, and another was terminated.

And time passed. Joseph was incarcerated in Pharaoh's prison for two more years, two more long years. By now his adolescence was behind him. He was a fully grown man, and though he had been immature beyond his years when he was a lad, he was mature beyond his years now that he was a man.

His brothers were far away, and even though he was in charge of everything in the prison, no one was bowing to him yet.

And the chief butler had forgotten him. Why does it seem so often to be a human quality to forget those who have done good things for us, and to remember those who have hurt us?

To remember Joseph would have been for the chief butler to recollect his time in prison, and it is a human tendency to turn away from reminders of pain or difficulty. I had a letter from a young friend telling me of her father's death and that one of the hardest things for her was her friends who said nothing. They did not know what to say, she wrote, and so they didn't say anything, and she found that she desperately needed some kind of response from them, any kind of response, but they were silent, and so she felt betrayed.

What is there to say? Only, "I love you, and I care," and sometimes we are afraid to say even that.

One of the hardest things for me after Hugh's death was meeting people for the first time and finding that they did not know what to say; they felt terribly uncomfortable, and I had to say the words for them, start talking naturally about Hugh. When people die they are not wiped out of our lives as though they had never been; they are still and always part of our history.

My friend's friends (and mine) were not being willingly insensitive to her needs. But we are embarrassed. Someone else's death is a *memento mori*, and we do not want to remember that we, too, will die. Most of us no longer have the old belief in literal pearly gates and golden streets. We no longer know what death means.

Last January I took my nineteen-year-old granddaughter, Charlotte, to north Florida with me, to stay with my friend, Pat, on one of the great tidal lakes. I wanted Charlotte to know something of her Florida roots, which go very deep. My mother's family settled in north Florida in the late fifteen hundreds with that first wave of French Huguenots—the very first settlers on this North American continent.

One day we drove out to Fleming's Island—and Fleming is one of my family names. There we went to Saint Margaret's Church, one of the charming little Carpenter Gothic churches to be found all over the South. To the side of and behind the church is an old cemetery, where some of my forbears are buried. It is a peaceful place, shaded from the sun by the great live oak trees, hung with Spanish moss. Azalea bushes were beginning to bud. The air was moist and warm. We wandered around, reading the inscriptions on the old tombstones. I had been there many times before, but it suddenly struck me that each one who had been buried there had been planted in the earth with the sure and certain assurance that the very body that had died would rise up again from the grave at the last day.

My grandfather, who died when he was 101, would not want to be resurrected in that ancient body. And I don't believe that he will be, nor that the specific bones, the flesh now long gone, will leap from the grave. When literalism about the resurrection of the body was what the Church taught, people could not be cremated, because God was not powerful enough to recreate anything from ashes.

Hugh was cremated because that was his wish, and I know that God is quite capable of doing anything the Creator wishes to do with Hugh's ashes, which are now scattered over his beloved garden. But the Church, by and large, has not grown into an understanding of a God who is not limited in what Love can do. So many people do not know what death means, and that is the cause of their embarrassment. My faith affirms that it means something, and I don't have to know what. I am confident in Paul's paradoxical phrase, "a spiritual body." Perhaps my "golden dreams" are a foretaste of what it may be like after death. I do not know. I only know that God will not forsake us, not now, not at the time of our death, not afterwards. Love does not create only to abandon or annihilate.

But the Church has not moved beyond the old literalism. In the Episcopal Church there are sometimes what are called "white funerals" where a white pall is used, and Easter hymns are sung, and it is all alleluia, alleluia, as though the crucifixion had never happened and we could jump right into Easter. After Hugh died it was a long time before I was able to say "Alleluia!" No matter how strong my faith that Hugh was still Hugh, growing in God's love, my grief still had to be gone through. Life without my beloved spouse was something I was not ready to shout "Alleluia" about.

My faith tells me that Hugh has gone on to a new challenge, to something new that God wants him to learn. We all have so much to learn—it can't possibly all be learned in one lifetime. That God has new lessons to teach us in one manner or other seems completely consistent with what Jesus taught. We don't have to know how God is going to do this; we only have to have faith.

For the ancient Hebrew the terror of Sheol was that it was outside God's memory, and if you are not in God's memory, you *are not*. Nothing is told us of what Jacob believed about Rachel after she died. Perhaps Jacob's grief continued so unremittingly because he did not believe in God's continuing concern for his creatures after death (it was a long time before the Hebrew began to conceive of the Resurrection when the Messiah should come, very much as we believe in it when Christ will come again).

But my faith about Rachel, about Hugh, must now be consistent with the metaphor of the universe as we understand it today (though our understanding of our metaphor may change or be made anew tomorrow), and that means that I have to be willing to live with open-ended questions. Many of the old certainties have been washed away. I think of that ancient Florida graveyard, and particularly of the small tombstones. Diphtheria, scarlet fever, and measles were great killers of small children, and it must have been comforting to believe that those beloved little bodies would one day rise again. I believe that, too, but with an unanswered question about *how*.

While Hugh was dying of cancer, so were two of my close friends, young women, in mid-life. Now Hugh's sister is dead from cancer. We seem to be surrounded by death.

But that has always been true. It was as true for Joseph as it is for any of us today. And there is more than one kind of death. Joseph had to die to his life as a pampered pet, and live a new life as a slave. He had to die to his life as Potiphar's overseer, and live in prison. I have had to die to my life as a married woman with a dearly loved husband, and live a new life which, while it is full and rich, is different, totally different.

Joseph's life as a prisoner came to an end.

And it came to pass at the end of two full years, that Pharaoh dreamed: and behold, he stood by the river. And behold, there came up out of the river seven well-favoured kine and fat-fleshed, and they fed in a meadow. And behold, seven other kine came up after them out of the river, ill-favoured and lean-fleshed; and stood by the other kine upon the brink of the river. And the ill-favoured and lean-fleshed kine did eat up the seven well-favoured and fat kine. So Pharaoh awoke.

And he slept and dreamed the second time, and behold, seven ears of corn came up upon one stalk, full and good. And behold, seven thin ears blasted with the east wind sprang up after them. And the seven thin ears devoured the seven full and good ears.

Pharaoh was troubled by these dreams, and he called for all his magicians and wise men, but nobody was able to interpret the dreams for him.

Then the chief butler, who had been in prison with Joseph, suddenly remembered him, and his interpretation of dreams, and told the Pharaoh about him. Pharaoh immediately sent for Joseph, who shaved himself, and changed his clothing, and was brought from the prison to Pharaoh.

Pharaoh told Joseph about his dream, and that no one could interpret it. *"But I have heard said of you that you can understand a dream and interpret it."*

Joseph answered Pharaoh as he had answered the butcher and the baker. *"It is not in me; it is God."* In this way we are told a good deal about what Joseph thought of God. Joseph in his short life had been through as much radical change as we have gone through in our understanding of Creation, and had been able to accept the change and learn from it.

Pharaoh told Joseph his dreams, and Joseph said, *"God has showed Pharaoh what he is about to do. The seven good kine are seven good years, and the seven good ears are seven years: the dream is one. And then seven thin and ill-favoured kine that came up after the seven years, and the seven empty ears blasted with the east wind shall be seven years of famine. This is the thing I have told Pharaoh: what God is going to do he has shown Pharaoh. There will be seven years of great plenty throughout all the land of Egypt, and after them shall arise seven years of famine, and the plenty shall be forgotten in the land of Egypt, and the famine will consume the land."*

Joseph continued by telling Pharaoh that because the dream was dreamed twice, it was a sign that it was established by God, and God would bring it to pass. So Joseph suggested that Pharaoh *"look for a man discreet and wise, and set him over the land of Egypt. Let Pharaoh do this, and let him appoint officers over the land, and take up the fifth part of the land of Egypt in the seven plenteous years. And let them gather all the food of those good years, and lay up corn under the hand of Pharaoh, and let them keep food in the cities. And that food shall be for store to the land against the seven years of famine which shall be in the land of Egypt, that the land perish not through the famine."*

We all know the familiar story. What Joseph said was appreciated by Pharaoh, who set Joseph over his house, as Potiphar had set Joseph over *his* house. But this time Joseph had authority over an entire land, the powerful land of Egypt. Pharaoh took off his own ring and put it on Joseph's hand, and dressed him royally, with a gold chain around his neck. He gave Joseph an Egyptian name, Zaphenath-Paneah (which fortunately we don't need to remember); he also gave him an Egyptian wife, Asenath, the daughter of the priest of On. So Joseph went out and surveyed all the land of Egypt.

And Joseph was thirty years old when he stood before Pharaoh, king of Egypt.

From prison to palace. Again it had happened.

From the favoured son of an old man to the victim of his brothers. From being sold into Egypt to Potiphar's steward. From steward to being the imprisoned victim of Potiphar's wife's lust. From prison to palace. Incredible reversals.

Most of our reversals are not nearly so dramatic.

Drama is easier than dailiness. Drama lends us a surge of adrenalin that gives us energy we didn't know we had. In the midst of crisis we are too busy to worry about ourselves or to indulge in self-pity.

It is never even hinted that Joseph whined or despaired during his long years in prison. The iron that was in his soul strengthened him. If ever he was in an iron collar it can't have been for long, since he took care of all the prisoners and all that went on in the prison. He managed to remain strong in spite of what must have been a tedious dailiness that we can hardly imagine.

In one of my reference books I read that Abraham left Ur in Chaldea around 2100 B.C. So if we go from Abraham to Isaac to Jacob to Joseph, Joseph must have lived around four thousand years ago. Two thousand years from Joseph to Jesus, two thousand years from Jesus to our own time.

* * *

A Prisoner

I know why I am here. I stole. I got in a fight and I killed a man. If ever it is right to take a man out of the light of day and put him in the dark of prison, it was right to put me here.

At night I dream, but I do not tell my dreams, for there is a man here (a prisoner, but in charge of us) who interprets dreams and says the interpreter is God. The butler, he said, would be restored to his former position, and the baker, he said, would lose his head.

And so I do not tell my dreams. I have lost enough without losing my head, too. But I have told him that I killed a man in a stupid quarrel.

I was punished justly, because I was getting what my deed deserved. But this man, this Joseph, has done nothing wrong.

I told him my story: I did not mean to kill. When I stole, I stole knowingly. I am an excellent thief. But knowingly I did not kill. It seems my hands still bear the stain of blood.

He listens to me. Quietly. He speaks words of neither condemnation nor excuse. He gives me work to do, to help him in the prison. I scrub the stone floors, and the water helps wash the blood from my hands. One night when a prisoner, an old man, is coughing his life away, Joseph has me stay with him. I hold the man high against my chest to ease his breathing. Why is he in prison, so fragile and so old? At dawn he dies in my arms and I hold him until his limbs begin to stiffen. After that, I am the one whom Joseph calls whenever death is near. Sometimes he stays with me, talking quietly to the prisoner leaving life. Sometimes I am alone.

I know that I will never kill again, and when Joseph leaves, sent for by Pharaoh, and does not return, I am given his place, put in charge of the prison.

I hope that Pharaoh treats him kindly.

Gad

a troop shall overcome him: but he shall
overcome at the last.

Genesis 49:19

Gad
7

BY GAD, there's not much to be known about Gad! How did his name get taken over as an expletive? Or was it simply a British pretense that one was not taking God's name in vain?

Gad was Zilpah's first son, Jacob's seventh. Moses describes Gad as a lioness and praises him for performing Yahweh's ordinances. But in the song of Deborah his tribe is chided for failing to participate in the war against Sisera. But Jacob encourages his son Gad, saying, *"he shall overcome at the last."*

By the time Joseph was established as principal ruler in Egypt, most of his older brothers would have been married and the fathers of children. But this story is Joseph's, and the others come into the story only because, at certain times, they affected Joseph.

Egypt stands in our minds for the fleshpots, the quick, good things of this life, instant gratification, fine foods, and wines, and clothing, and luxurious housing. Four hundred years later, the Hebrew children escaped

Pharaoh and were heading back to the Promised Land, and God sustained them with manna, the sweet, flaky substance that fell each day from the sky. But they complained that they were tired of this manna, that they longed for their onions and garlic and all the fresh foods they were accustomed to in Egypt. Slavery began to seem preferable to freedom as long as slavery kept them comfortable.

It is all right to enjoy the "creature comforts" as long as they are not paramount, as long as they do not become little gods, as long as we do not become slaves to them. What God created is good, very good, and to be enjoyed, as long as we never forget the Source.

Joseph never scorned the fleshpots when they were offered to him. He wore with flair his coat of many colours, though it became a sign of favouritism rather than simply a beautiful and comfortable garment. More honestly, he enjoyed the luxuries of Potiphar's palace and the far greater luxuries showered on him by Pharaoh. But when his luxuries were taken away he did not whine and whimper. The fact that he told both the baker and the Pharaoh that the interpretation of dreams comes from God, not from himself, tells us clearly that Joseph had not forgotten God, that the fleshpots were not of prime importance in his life.

Jesus enjoyed eating with his friends, enjoyed the good things (and was criticized for it by the moral majority). And it is all right for us to enjoy them, too, as long as we remember that all good and lovely things come from our Maker, even if we have prepared or crafted them: well-cooked meals, finely-carved furniture, embroidered linens. And our enjoyment should be an act of worship. My friend Tallis was talking to a Quaker friend about the Eucharist, and how important it was to him. The Eucharist and the other sacraments are not part of Quaker worship, yet the old lady gently replied that she never sat down to a meal without thinking of the body and blood of the Lord, and giving thanks.

The evening meal, the table set with the best china and crystal, and lit by candles, has always been sacramental for me, the focal point of the day. It is when the family gathers together, shares the day's events, and God's bounty. When our children were little I did not mind *when* we ate as long as we ate together. If Hugh was previewing a Broadway play we sometimes ate at five o'clock. If someone had an after-school project we ate at eight or eight thirty. The family dinner table is no longer tradition in many families today; it is a great loss.

Now the dinner table is very different. In New York, where I stay during the academic year, I am living with my granddaughter, Charlotte, who is in college. Often one of her friends is living with us, too, for months at a time. But the dinner table, the candles, the food prepared with love, are still important.

When I am at Crosswicks, my son, Bion, is the cook. His wife, Laurie, is a busy physician and never knows when she is going to get home, so Bion has taken over the cooking, and a marvelous and inventive cook he is, coming up with delicious new recipes for the late summer overflow from the garden. As the days grow shorter towards summer's end we still eat out, by kerosene lamp light, and we stay out to watch the stars. Across the fields are the woods and then the ancient hills—*"from whence cometh my help."*

When I was in Jerusalem it was the hills which deeply moved me, helping me to understand better than ever before the 121st psalm. How many people throughout the centuries have looked towards the hills for help, hills that are a metaphor of the strong, steadfast love of God. Hills are also a metaphor for the right and proper expression of grief, of directing our loss and anguish to God. All during my life I have slowly learned about grief, and the appropriate expression of it. Wearing mourning in the old days was not such a bad idea, because it took into visible account the fact of death, which we now try to hide (even in the Church we try to hide it) so that it won't embarrass others.

Joseph, despite all his power and prestige, despite his Egyptian wife, still had loss and grief to work through. He was still far from home and family, and from the familiar. He had had to learn a new language, a new way of daily living, which included being isolated when he ate. In spite of all his power and wealth, there was still discrimination, for the Egyptians would not eat with a Hebrew. How lonely for him to have to eat alone, always alone! Is this not something like Southerners allowing their children to be suckled by a black wet nurse, and yet refusing to eat at the same table with the woman who nourished their little ones?

Perhaps this is one reason that Joseph's immense secular power did not go to his head. Perhaps, despite wealth and luxury, he knew moments of feeling forsaken. Like all the biblical heroes (like all of us human creatures) he was complex, capable of feeling opposite emotions simultaneously.

Meanwhile there were, as Joseph had told Pharaoh there would be, seven years of plenty, and during this time of prosperity Joseph laid up food from the countryside for all the cities, storing it so that there would be enough laid by for the seven years of famine. Certainly he had enough work to do, and little time to brood. We are not told a great deal about his home life, whether or not he loved and was loved by the wife Pharaoh had chosen for him. Despite the love stories of Isaac and Rebecca, Jacob and Rachel, arranged marriages were then the custom for both Hebrew and Egyptian. Joseph had two sons by Asenath; the first son was called Manasseh, who remains a mysterious character throughout Scripture. The second son Joseph named Ephraim, saying, *"For God has called me to be fruitful in the land of my affliction."*

So, even in the midst of his worldly success, Joseph still thought of Egypt as the land of his affliction. Did he ever, on the journey into Egypt, or during his years in prison, cry out, *"My God, my God, why have you forsaken me!"*? That has been the human cry of anguish throughout the centuries. The psalmist cries it in the 22nd psalm. Jesus cried it out on the cross, and in so doing freed us all to cry it in moments of deepest pain and loss.

The night of the day we learned that Hugh had cancer I turned, as always, to the strength-giving of Evening Prayer, and the first psalm for that evening was the 22nd, *"My God, my God, why have you forsaken me?"*

I was not at home, but a few miles away, at a conference centre. The onset of Hugh's illness was so sudden that there was no time to find a replacement for me, and the centre was close enough to the hospital that I could commute. But the blow that it was cancer had come only that afternoon, and I felt raw with shock. I read those anguished words in a strange room, with my world turned upside down, those words that Jesus, too, cried out. And so, despite the pain, they brought me strength.

The words of the psalmist. The words of Jesus. They are incredibly personal words, and they cannot be spoken by one who is not there.

But Joseph, as far as we know, did not question but accepted the afflictions that came upon him as he accepted the power. So he laid up provision for the time of dearth, knew his wife, begat sons, ate alone, did what had to be done.

And the seven years of plenteousness in the land of Egypt were ended. And the seven years of dearth began to come, as Joseph had said they would, but in all the land of Egypt there was bread.

And when all the land of Egypt was famished, the people cried to Pharaoh for bread, and Pharaoh said to all the Egyptians, "Go to Joseph and do whatever he tells you to do."

And the famine was over all the face of the earth, and Joseph opened all the storehouses and sold to the Egyptians. And all countries came into Egypt to Joseph to buy corn, because the famine was terrible in all lands.

Our planet is once again suffering from famine. Not only is there drought and famine in Africa, with the dry sand of the Sahara gradually taking over more and more of the fertile land, but our own southeast and western states have experienced terrible drought. We may not have had a Joseph, but perhaps he taught us something, for, in a gesture of fraternal compassion, farmers whose crops produced grain and wheat in abundance sent to those whose crops were withering. The response of the world to the horrible plight of the Armenians after the earthquake and to Bangladesh after its flood, is proof that our human hearts are still warm, despite the coldness which presses in on every side.

Famine and disease. Yes, there was famine, but there is little mention of disease in Genesis. People died of old age; women too often died in childbirth. There is no mention of cancer, or even of head colds. Men and women were sexually and healthily active, enjoying each other into old age.

But today AIDS is reaching disastrously epidemic proportions in Africa, hitting men, women, children. Someone told me that the virus has been found in mosquitoes—a terrifying thought. It is increasing in this country. Although contaminated hypodermic needles account for many cases, the most common cause is intercourse.

The sexual revolution has backfired. We needed to move from the old repressions, the unscriptural idea that nice women did not enjoy sex, and that therefore men had to have a separate standard. But, as almost always happens, the pendulum has swung too far, swinging from repression to undisciplined lust.

How do we find love, that love which God showed us in Jesus? How do we return to ourselves as observers and contemplators of God's Creation? Not only can men not have a separate standard, but not one of us can separate ourselves from any part of God's Creation.

Perhaps the Egypt into which Joseph was sold needed a new morality as much as we do, but it must be a *new* morality, not a return to the old, which wasn't very moral. Some pretty scandalous things happened among those eminent Victorians. And in our own time scandal has soiled the souls and reputations of prominent Christians. We need to understand that love never treats subject as object. Indeed, treating subject as object is the beginning of pornography.

As I observe and contemplate love, it is never self-righteous. It does not condemn. It is a sacrifice, a sacred and hallowed giving. I have received this love and been allowed to give it, and this is why, rather than by accident of birth, I am a Christian.

And Joseph, despite the pantheon of gods with which he was surrounded, was able to retain his faith in the One God of his people.

But such faith is a mystery. The phrase about God which means the most to me is the *mysterium tremendum et fascinans*. It doesn't translate well: the tremendous and fascinating mystery. It does better in Latin.

Joseph, having been purged in the fire, knew God to be a total mystery. There was a purity, a directness, to faith in the Creator before the coming of the Law; it was a smaller world than that of the Exodus and the journey to the Promised Land. And by the time of Jesus both the world and the law had become overcomplicated. The law was by now so cumbersome that it was almost impossible to get through a day without inadvertently breaking some jot or tittle of it, and John the Baptist, with his cry for repentance, was offering relief from the tangled web of Law that had become laws.

But for Joseph there were the stars at night, the sands of the desert, the wild winds, and mystery. We, too, are mysteries, and we cannot be explained, we creatures who are born to observe and contemplate, any more than the Maker of it all can be explained.

Hugo Rahner writes,

Without mystery all religion must wither into barren rationalism. The church alone has retained the element of mystery: by her sacraments she has consecrated sun, moon, water, bread, wine, and oil, and also the love of the flesh, nor will it ever be permitted to her to cease teaching mankind that behind the veils of the visible the eternal secrets lie concealed, and that it is only through the word of God which lives on in the church that we can recognize the true meaning of earthly things.

Because I do not believe that Jesus ever had denominations or a divided Christendom in mind, when I speak of "the Church" I refer to all of us, from the sects to the fundamentalists to the Pentecostals to the main-line Protestants to the Catholics to—to all of us. That we are still one Church despite all our divisions is also a mystery.

Unless we are able to accept mystery we will not be able to move beyond literalism into a living faith, a trusting that a God of love will not create and then abandon or annihilate.

Carrying my babies was a marvelous mystery, lives growing unseen except by the slow swelling of my belly and the delightful stirrings within. Death is an even greater mystery.

After Hugh's death many people asked me if I still talk to him. And my reply is always, "No, I don't want to hold him back." For I think we can do that, clinging to the beloved who has died, rather than allowing freedom to go on and do whatever it is that God has waiting and prepared for husband, or wife, or child, or friend.

Hugh will always be with me, part of me. Inevitably he comes up in daily conversation. There is no way I can talk without including him. We were together for well over half our lives. But his mortal body is gone and I don't know what God has in store for him now.

But it is even more mysterious than that. In God's universe we are never completely separated from any part of it.

So while I do not want to hold Hugh back (from whatever God is calling him to do and be and become) so I also know that he is still part of God's purpose.

On the anniversary of his death I was carefully scheduled to be away from home, having accepted three speaking jobs in Michigan. This, I hoped, would keep my children from worrying about me, and I knew that I would be better off if I was busy, and doing work I hoped had some value.

The first stop was Calvin College. My friend Marilyn from Niles, Michigan was with me, and we were put up in the Harley Hotel in Grand Rapids, where there were real glasses to drink out of, not plastic, and good quality tissues. I stay in many hotels on my travels and that is one way of grading them.

The second stop, the "two-night stand," was Spring Arbor College, and we were put up at a Knight's Inn in Jackson. Marilyn got out of her car, went into the room she had been assigned, and came out with a strange look on her face. Then she went into my room, which was next door, and came out, still with that strange look, and called me to come.

I went into a room smelling heavily of sweetish antiseptic. There was bright red carpeting on the floor, a bright purple velvet bedspread on the bed, bright purple velvet curtains at the windows, and on the walls were murals of windows with chartreuse shutters. Marilyn assured me that her room was identical. There were only two things to do in that room when we weren't at the college: sleep, and write. I had with me the manuscript of this book, and I was working on it dutifully, and without enthusiasm. I had promised the book to Luci Shaw, and I care about keeping promises. But working without enthusiasm is not my usual way.

And then it was as though I heard Hugh saying to me, "You know you don't want to work on *Sold Into Egypt* right now. What you want to work on is that fantasy you've been thinking about. Go ahead and write it." So I put *Sold Into Egypt* aside, and that day, and the next, I wrote at white heat whenever I was free to be in the room. I wrote twenty-eight pages. And continued when we went on to Sturgess and were radically upgraded to a Holiday Inn.

An Acceptable Time was the book I had to write then.

I didn't hear Hugh's physical voice. I didn't see him. But I felt him, his *is*ness, with me, at a time when my grief was raw. The night before, sitting in that red and purple room and reading Evening Prayer with Marilyn, the words of the Psalms almost made me break down. My body, my spirit, all of me was aware of and open to Hugh. I don't want to make too much of this. All I know was that it happened and it was a great and beneficent gift.

Perhaps a mere year after my husband's death was too soon for me to be thinking about all the theological issues of life and death that the story of Joseph demands. Certainly I believed that Hugh still *was*, *is*, and I still believe that. Perhaps I needed to work on the fantasy, with its themes of love and sacrifice, to help me understand Joseph, and to relax in the promise of Jesus' love and sacrifice.

Several people said to me, "At least you know that Hugh is happy now."

How do I know that? Happiness is not always for our greatest good. It may be that God has more joyful—or more difficult—or more challenging and wonderful work for Hugh to do. I don't have to know whether or not Hugh is *happy*. I need to know only that he is growing in God's love.

This past year almost everywhere I have spoken, someone has asked me, "What do you think of reincarnation?" The question is asked sometimes with fear, sometimes with hope, sometimes accusingly.

Perhaps the question of reincarnation has come to the forefront of people's thinking about life and death because the Church has held back, unable to move from the thinking of my forbears in St. Margaret's graveyard on Fleming's Island in north Florida. Some churches remain stuck in the old literal representations of heaven and hell, so graphically painted by Hieronymus Bosch. They are still good metaphors, but no longer to be taken literally, anymore than the Aristotelian sandwich of heaven, earth, hell, is to be taken literally.

When the Church is silent, other voices inevitably are heard.

Thoughts about what life after death holds for us should never be a refuge from the fear of death. Who knows what the God of love has in store for us? There are many important lessons to be learned before we are ready for the unveiled glory of the Presence.

But is this one life we are given not enough? Hugh lived the biblical three score years and ten. Surely we need not ask for more. But what about God's children who do not have lives of any real quality? What about the ten-year-old o.d.ed on drugs? The raped and murdered adolescent? The children starving in Africa, or India, or South America? Or the little ones in St. Margaret's graveyard, dead at only a few years of age from scarlet fever or diphtheria? Doesn't God want more for them than that?

In the 22nd psalm we read, *"To him (God) alone all who sleep in the earth bow down in worship; all who go down to the dust fall before him."* So even in the dust of the grave we worship God. What God created will not be left unfinished.

Why are so many Christians afraid of the idea that the God of love will continue to care for us? There are hints all through Scripture. In the Psalms: *"Before you were formed in the womb I knew you,"* (echoing Jeremiah). *"In my house are many mansions,"* Jesus assured, each one prepared to meet the need of each person after death. There is nothing inconsistent with Christianity in such considerations as long as we don't fall into idolatry.

I hope this does not sound like what is called New Age-ism, of which many Christians seem to be terribly afraid. I am not a New Ager, and I don't know a great deal about this movement. The chief problem seems to me to be that old heresy, Pelagianism—thinking we can do it all ourselves. At its worst it is the belief that because we can do it ourselves we don't need God.

And it is, perhaps, an indictment of the Church which has allowed God's wonder to be tarnished, which is fearful rather than joyful, and which has forgotten the wonderful wildness of Jesus, who could spit on the dust and make a blind man see, who could tell a little girl to arise from death, and who loved his disciples despite their betrayal of him, as Joseph also was called to love his brothers.

I know that I need God, and that if we are to care for the precarious ecology of this planet it will only be with our hands in the hand of God. That we do nothing, accomplish nothing, without God. After I had spent several days speaking in Fort Wayne, Indiana, first for the Friends of the Library, then for the Episcopal Church, a man who had not come to any of my talks wrote a letter to the editor of the local paper accusing me of being "a self-professed New Ager." What made him tell this bald-faced lie, after which he went on to accuse my books (without having read them) of being unChristian, leading children down the path to perdition? What is this fear that causes "Christians" to vilify and attack other Christians blindly? Aren't Christians supposed to act out of love, not fear? Aren't we supposed to be recognized by our love for one another? Does not our faith in the Lord of the universe keep us safe in Christ? Does not perfect love banish fear?

And what am I to do about my instinctive reaction towards people who are judgmental? How do I, in my turn, keep from being judgmental? I know that I frequently err. But at least I don't want those who disagree with me damned to eternal hell. I do want us all to meet with love at the Heavenly Banquet.

I don't worry much about reincarnation one way or another. It is enough for me to believe that God's love never ends. I don't need to know how God is caring for Hugh now, only that Hugh is still alive in God, as much as I am alive in God.

Elizabeth Kubler-Ross says that the subconscious mind cannot conceive of its own extinction. Most of the time the conscious mind cannot, either. We know that we are going to die, but most of the time we don't believe it.

There is a theory that people have to finish working out unresolved relations with each other until love is perfected. How that is going to be brought about is in the hands of the Maker, and I am willing to leave it in the realm of mystery, in the design of the *mysterium tremendum et fascinans*. Faith is not for the things we can prove, but for the things we cannot prove.

The medical profession is in a time of crisis because of its amazing new technology. There are instruments and techniques that are wonderful lifesavers; some of them are also terrible death prolongers. The church is in its own time of crisis, seeming to fall into the same trap as the scientists, that of attempting to prolong the life of the body even when the spirit is gone.

The early people of Genesis did not have to face such ethical dilemmas. They lived to ripe old ages without the benefit of medicine. They were robust and healthy as long as the land yielded to them its grain and wine and oil, its milk and honey and olives. In times of famine people died of starvation—but not as many as are dying of starvation today, because it was a much less crowded planet.

The famine against which Joseph had stored up great reserves of grain spread far beyond Egypt, and when Jacob learned that there was food to be bought in Egypt he sent his ten eldest sons to go buy corn. Benjamin, his youngest son, he kept at home, fearing something might happen to him, as he believed had happened to Joseph.

And the irony of it was that it was Joseph himself who was in complete charge of dispensing food to the hungry, so it was to their own brother (though of course they had no idea of this, thinking Joseph long dead) that Jacob's sons applied. After the long trek to Egypt, the ten of them prostrated themselves before him, like the sheaves of corn, like the stars of his dreams. They prostrated themselves before this magnificent stranger dressed in fine clothes and wearing all the emblems of power.

And Joseph saw his brothers and he knew them, but made himself strange to them, and spoke roughly to them, and said to them, "From where do you come?"

And they said, "From the land of Canaan to buy food."

And Joseph recognized his brothers, but they did not recognize him.

Did Joseph have any expectation that his brothers would come to Egypt, looking for food? How strange, after all these years, to see these ten men, some of them middle-aged by now. How did he recognize them? From a family resemblance to Jacob? If he suspected that they might come, for the famine was bad in Canaan, that very expectation would have made it easier for Joseph to recognize them, those brothers who had been so jealous of him that they had plotted against him; some of them had even been eager to kill him. Paradoxically, he had both suffered and prospered because of them. But surely by now he would have seen and acknowledged his own part in what had happened, his arrogance, his insufferable bragging. He had brought at least some of his problems upon himself.

And Joseph (seeing his brothers prostrate before him) *remembered the dreams which he had dreamed and he said to them, "You are spies, and have come to see the nakedness of this land."*

And they said, "No, my Lord, your servants are twelve brothers, the sons of one man in Canaan, and the youngest is at home with our father, and one of us is not."

But Joseph repeated the accusation that they were spies, and said that the only way that they could prove that they were honest men was to bring their youngest brother to him. He would keep one of them hostage in Egypt, in prison, as surety, while they went back to Canaan for Benjamin. Meanwhile, he locked them all up for three days.

To have time to think. To decide what to do. Was revenge totally sweet, or was it bittersweet? Egypt was still the land of his exile. He longed for home.

At the end of three days Joseph brought his brothers out of prison, and again told them that one of them should be bound in prison (as Joseph had been bound). The others were to go and buy corn to relieve the famine at home, then go back and give food to their father. Then they were to bring Benjamin to Joseph.

"So shall your story be verified, and you shall not die."

The ten brothers huddled in consternation, admitting one to another that they had been truly guilty about Joseph—and that was why this present distress had fallen upon them, with this strange lord standing by, darting glances at them.

And Reuben answered them, saying, "Didn't I beg you not to sin against the child? And you would not hear. Therefore his blood must be avenged." And they did not know that Joseph understood them, because he spoke to them through an interpreter.

At last Joseph was hearing his own language, words that must have shaken him, but he held himself back, speaking only in the language of Egypt. By now he would have been completely fluent in Egyptian, perhaps even dreaming in that language (as occasionally I used to dream in French), but the language of his birth, coming from his brothers, must have pierced him with homesickness. *And he turned himself away from them and wept.*

He was to do considerably more weeping before finally the twelve brothers were reconciled, and Jacob was to see all his sons together again.

Men in Joseph's day were not afraid to weep, had not yet been forced by society to repress honest emotion. I am glad that Joseph wept, because it meant that he was not concerned only with revenge, but also for his brothers, concerned for little Benjamin, not so little any more, concerned for his father, who must be an old man by now.

I have wept for the loss of my husband, wept with our children, wept alone, wept in my bed at home, and sometimes in strange beds in hotel rooms. During the years of our marriage Hugh and I sometimes wept together, holding each other, not tears of self-indulgence or self-pity, but tears which are an appropriate response to the sorrows and losses of this world.

Joseph wept.

Jesus wept.

The shortest verse in the Bible is *Jesus wept*.

Why did he weep?

He wept after his friend, Lazarus, had died, and before he had raised him from the dead. The people said that he wept because he loved Lazarus so, and that was probably one of the reasons.

My friend Tallis says that Jesus wept from sheer anguished frustration, because nobody understood what he was about, nobody, not one of his disciples, not one of his friends. He may have held on to the hope that Mary would understand, Mary who had washed his feet with rare oil and wiped them with her hair. But even Mary did not understand.

And perhaps, because of the paradox of Jesus being human as well as God, he wept because of the anguish of his mission. He knew that he was the Messiah, and yet he also knew that when he went to Jerusalem he would be captured and killed.

And he wept because of Lazarus, but not because Lazarus was dead. He had stayed away from Bethany to be sure that Lazarus was indeed dead. By the time Jesus got there Lazarus had been dead for four days. Martha, that blunt woman, put it graphically: *"Lord, by this time he stinketh."*

Lazarus had been dead for four days, had been for four days in the Presence, and Jesus had to bring him back from that bliss. And so he wept for Lazarus. Then he had the stone rolled away and called him back to mortality.

We don't know much about Lazarus after his raising. Once when Jesus came to Bethany Lazarus was there at dinner with Mary and Martha, and people came to stare. But it would seem that he was different after Jesus brought him back to life, still partly in the presence of God, homesick for heaven. And it was likely that he had to go into hiding because he, like Jesus, was sought by the confused and angry authorities.

Jesus wept.

The tears of Jesus dignify our own tears. I am grateful for that brief, two-word verse of Scripture, because it frees us to weep our own legitimate tears. When we are alone with God there is no need to put on a front.

Jesus wept.

Joseph wept.

Gad. We don't know what Gad thought about God. But Gad grew up in the over-arching shadow of the patriarchs, Abraham, Isaac, and Jacob, the father of the twelve sons. They knew themselves to be called, specially called.

And one thing I learned in working on the fantasy which needed to be written before this book is that Gad was never separated from Christ; that Christ, the second Person of the Trinity, has always been, is always, and always will be available to all people and at all times. We are so focussed on the Incarnation, on Jesus of Nazareth, that sometimes we forget that the Second Person of the Trinity didn't just arrive two thousand years ago, but has always been. Christ was the Word that shouted all of Creation into being, all the galaxies and solar systems, all the subatomic particles, and the wonderful mix of Creation that is what makes up each one of us.

Jesus said, to the horror of the establishment people, *Before Abraham was, I am.*

In Chapter 20 of Luke's gospel Jesus has been questioned by the elders of the temple, who are trying to trick him. Finally he says, *"How is it that they say the Christ is the Son of David? David himself declares in the Book of Psalms, 'The Lord said to my Lord, Sit at my right hand, until I make your enemies a footstool for your feet.' David calls him 'Lord.' How can he then be his son?"*

Another heresy down the drain, I hope. How can we blithely assign all those who lived before Jesus to the flames of eternal hell when they never denied Christ? Their way of knowing was inevitably different from ours, but God cannot be limited, and a God of love does not casually wipe out the prophets and the people who found Christ in the love of the Creator.

Paul talks about the journey from Egypt to the Promised Land, and the Rock that went before the people, *and that rock was Christ.*

So, for Gad, for Joseph, for Moses, for all of us, Christ always *is.*

My Christmas poem for this year runs:

He came, quietly impossible,
Out of a young girl's womb,
A love as amazingly marvelous
As his bursting from the tomb.

This child was fully human,
This child was wholly God.
The hands of All Love fashioned him
Of mortal flesh and bone and blood,

The ordinary so extraordinary
The stars shook in the sky

As the Lord of all the universe
Was born to live, to love, to die.

He came, quietly impossible:
Nothing will ever be the same:
Jesus, the Light of every heart—
The God we know by Name.

But we find it hard to hold on to the impossible, so we tend to settle for the limited possible. And our vision of God dwindles, and we become selfish and hard of heart as we close ourselves off from love.

Gad's Wife

Had I known what a strange family I was marrying into I would have fought the match all the way. I thought I was marrying Gad. Instead I married Gad and his eleven brothers, including the one who was dead, torn into pieces by wild beasts—though I thought Gad's expression strange as I was told this.

I do not mean that the brothers came to our tent or did anything unseemly. In fact, Simeon and Levi scarcely spoke to me, as though the wives of the sons of the slaves were less important than the wives of the other brothers. What I mean is that Gad was not Gad except as part of his brothers. The father, Jacob, and the brothers and their wives were the tribe. There was nobody else. They had their tribal god, and I was expected to abandon my home goddess and obey their god. Since their god never bothered me, that was all right, and nobody knew what I was doing when I left the tent to watch the moon rise, or suggested the best times for plantings.

My prayers were answered, and I gave Gad sons. And then, for myself and my own joy, I had daughters. I do not mean to complain. Gad was good to me, a vigorous lover and a good provider. And though his pride was in his sons he loved our little girls and played with them and made them laugh. But sons were what counted. How strange! How could a man have sons without a woman? But if Gad and his brothers thought of women at all, it was because they were useful as producers of men. And, of course, to keep tent, draw water, be available whenever desire arose.

We had, I suppose, a good life. My children had plenty of cousins as playmates as well as each other, and in their games no difference was made between the grandchildren of the two slave women and the grandchildren of the two wives.

Gad was the first son of Zilpah, the slave who was unloved Leah's maid. She was less well thought of than Bilhah, dead Rachel's maid.

Dead Rachel. Dead Joseph. Not dead to Father Jacob! They were ever present in his brooding eyes, in the downtwist of his mouth when he thought he was alone. Sometimes he would clutch Benjamin—my youngest brother-in-law, still smooth of cheek—clutch him so hard that the poor lad would squirm and try to break away. Benjamin, the beloved. The rest of the brothers are—sons. Father Jacob has sons, as he has camels and goats and sheep. He knows how to breed well, both man and beast.

He has grandsons. Oh, yes, he has grandsons. Between us, we have given him plenty, and granddaughters, too, and Reuben's children are old enough to give their grandfather great-grandsons and daughters.

He will like that. Sometimes I wonder why he does not collect gods as he collects the rest of his livestock. Between us, we would give him quite a few.

But I do not mean to be unkind. He is good to us, the old patriarch.

But what, I wonder, happened to Dinah, the one sister? Where is she? Benjamin asked me about her, once, telling me she had been his mother—or like his mother—after Rachel died giving birth to him. He loved Dinah, but even he does not know where she is, or why she is not with the rest of the family.

When I leave the tent to watch the moon rise I pray for Dinah. I pray that she was not sent away from home by men who do not understand the ways of women. There is a mystery about Dinah that in some way touches on Simeon and Levi, whose faces close in on the rare occasions that her name is spoken. I pray that she may have left the home tents for love of some man who will be good to her, and let her have her own home god, if that is what she wants.

But I will never know.

Asher

his bread is rich;
he provides fruit fit for a king.

Genesis 49:20

Asher

8

WHEN JACOB GIVES HIS BLESSINGS to his sons, he says, *"Asher, his bread is rich, he provides fruit fit for a king."* Asher's land was lush and productive, and he benefited from his geography.

Moses, in his blessing, says, *"Most blessed of the sons may Asher be! Let him be privileged among his brothers and bathe his feet in oil!"*

And after all this we still don't know a great deal about Asher, Zilpah's second son, Jacob's eighth. In Egypt, how did Asher feel when Joseph wept? Did he see that the great man was turning away because he had tears in his eyes? Or were the brothers too terrified by all that was happening to notice anything except that the great man thought they were spies, and was holding one of them in Egypt while the others went to fetch Benjamin? It was fearful and confusing. Why did the most powerful man in Egypt want their little brother? (Not so little any more. By now, Benjamin was fully grown.)

Joseph wept.

One of the most important things we can do for each other in times of grief is to weep together. Words are useless. We are in the realm of ultimate mystery. Nothing speaks except touch and tears.

And, sometimes, anger. When Mrs. Pat Campbell's son was killed in the trenches in World War I, George Bernard Shaw wrote to her, his beloved friend, starting the letter with "Damn damn damn damn damn." That was compassionate understanding, outrage at the blasphemy of war. It was not sacrilegious, and was far more acceptable to God, I believe, than pious utterances about its being God's will. Such "piosity" is an obscenity, not a comfort. Terrible things are not God's will, but God can enter them with redemptive love, that is the promise of the Incarnation.

Was Joseph ever able to weep with his wife, Asenath? He was not allowed to eat with her, since she was an Egyptian and he a Hebrew, although he was allowed to sleep with her, know her, give her children. Did he ever weep in her arms?

I visualize Joseph turned away from his brothers, his shoulders shaking a little (did they think he was laughing at them?), his hand covering his face until he could turn and look at them again.

A formidable figure, this Joseph, with the power to hold Simeon in Egypt. (Since Simeon was one of the two brothers who had murdered Shechem, that may have had something to do with Joseph's choice of hostage.)

Joseph sent off the other nine brothers for home, ordering his servants to make sure that not only should their sacks be filled with corn, but that their money should be returned to them—the money with which they had paid for the corn—and put in their sacks.

On their way home, when one of the brothers, we are not told which one, *opened his sack to give his ass provender at the inn, he saw the money, because it was right in the mouth of the sack.*

And he said to his brothers, "My money is returned; look, it is in my sack!" and their hearts failed them, and they were afraid, saying one to another, what is this that God has done to us?"

Was it Levi who found the money? Did he and Simeon think of God when they slaughtered Shechem and his tribe? Were the brothers thinking of God when they planned to kill Joseph? When they sold him into Egypt?

When they got home they told their father all that had happened, how the lord of the land spoke roughly to them and accused them of being spies, despite their protestations that they were simply *"twelve brothers, sons of our father; one is not, and the youngest is this day with our father in the land of Canaan."*

They also told their father that the lord of Egypt had informed them that the only way they could prove their innocence was by leaving Simeon in jail until they brought their youngest brother, Benjamin, to Egypt. Then and then only would the great lord believe that the brothers were not spies, and Simeon would be restored to them.

Jacob put his arms around Benjamin in anguish, holding, shielding the beloved flesh of his youngest son.

The brothers had opened only one of their sacks on their way home. Now they opened the others, and each one of them found that his bag of money was in his sack, and they were afraid, and so was Jacob. He wailed, *"You are robbing me of my children. Joseph is no more. Simeon is no more. And now you want to take Benjamin. All this I must bear."*

Again it was Reuben who intervened. He promised his father the lives of his own two sons if he did not bring Benjamin back to him. *"Put him in my care and I will bring him back to you."*

It was a generous and rash offer. Reuben did not ask his wife, he simply made this wild promise. But it was not enough for Jacob. He cried, *"My son is not going down with you, for now his brother is dead and he is the only one left to me. If anything should happen to him on the way, you would bring down my grey hairs with sorrow to the grave."*

Benjamin alone is left to me! Reuben turned away. Benjamin alone? What about the other ten? Was it only for his beloved Rachel's children that Jacob truly cared?

Jacob was too involved in his own grief to understand what he was doing to his sons. And by now perhaps they were used to being second-best. They all lived near their father, with their wives and children, and they lived well. Their flocks had increased, and, until the famine struck their gardens had grown, their fields and flocks had prospered. They knew themselves to have *a goodly heritage.*

But Jacob was still immersed in grief, grief for Rachel, for Joseph he thought to be dead. He could not bear any more death. What did he believe about Rachel? About Joseph? About his fathers, Isaac and Abraham?

In the creed, as I say it each day, I affirm that "I believe in the resurrection of the body." I don't need to belabour my expressed belief that we don't know how that body is going to be resurrected, or what it is going to be like. If Paul could believe in a *spiritual body* so, most of the time, can I. It is yet another mystery of the Word made flesh.

The Episcopal Church is a credal church. When I go to the Congregational Church near Crosswicks there is no creed, but there is an "Affirmation of Faith." Wheaton College requires its faculty to sign a "Statement of Faith," and I can't see much difference between creeds and affirmations and statements. By whatever name it is called, most religious establishments express what they believe in one way or another. And these expressions are all inadequate. What we hold in common is the affirmation of our faith in the mystery of the Word made flesh.

If that Word should come to another planet in another galaxy with different life forms, and be made manifest according to the flesh of that planet, this different incarnation would still be the same original Word made flesh. That Word may express itself in many images, many languages, each equally the true Word.

We are given a unique glimpse of the mystery of the Word in the wonder of the Transfiguration, when briefly James and John and Peter were allowed to see the radiance of their Lord, bright and glistening and wholly other. Is that how we will appear at our resurrection?

We are given further glimpses when we remember that after the Resurrection Jesus was never recognized by sight, though he ate fish with his disciples, shared their bread and wine, to prove that the resurrection body was true body.

David Steindl-Rast reminds us that the word *spirit* means *breath*, and that breath stands for life, so to be spiritual means to be alive. The spiritual body that Paul talks about is a real body that is truly alive—truly aware, truly being—as most of us are alive only occasionally.

Did Jacob have any such hope? We don't know. But he rebelled categorically at the idea of letting Benjamin go to

Egypt. His roars are like that of the psalmist many generations later. *"I will say to the God of my strength, 'Why have
you forsaken me? All day long they mock me and say, Where is
now your God?' "*

I, too, have cried out with the psalmist, *"You are the
God of my strength; why have you put me away from you?"*

There was no hesitation in Old Testament days about
crying out to the Lord in times of trouble. *"Awake, O Lord!
Why are you sleeping? Arise! Do not reject us forever. Why
have you hidden your face and forgotten our affliction and
oppression?"*

In the 13th psalm the appeal is even stronger: *"How
long, O LORD? Will you forget me forever? How long will you
hide your face from me? How long must I wrestle with my
thoughts and every day have sorrow in my heart? How long
will my enemy triumph over me?"*

I do not believe that God is ever absent from us. There
may be times when God's face seems hidden, but if we
know where to look, it's always there.

There have been many times, such as the captivity out
of which the psalmist was crying, and often in the world's
history, and in our own personal histories, when we cry
out like the psalmist. And in our crying out we try to
come to terms with whatever it is that is troubling us
("No! Benjamin shall not go!"), and we struggle to be
human.

We make a terrible error when we think that to be
human means to be perfect, some kind of unerring Christian model that cannot exist in reality. Only God is perfect.
To be human is to be able to laugh, to cry, to live fully, to
be aware of our lives as we are living them. We are the
creatures *who know that we know*, unlike insects who live
by unthinking instinct. That ability to think, to know, to
reflect, to question, marks us as human beings. And our

humanness includes an awareness that we are mortal. To be a human being is to be born, to live, to die. We have a life span. George Macdonald reminds us that Jesus came to us in a human body not so that he would be like us, but so that we would be like Jesus. Jesus died to his human life, and what he demands of us is equally hard, never sentimental or easy, and it is always part of that call to be human.

We don't know what Jesus looked like, but it's a pretty safe guess that he didn't look like most greeting-card representations of him; it is not likely that he was a blue-eyed blond. He was a Jew, and he was a carpenter. He was a strong, rough-hewn man.

Dr. Paul Brand tells of a time when he was a student in England and his aunt went in to London to hear a famous speaker. She came back absolutely shattered because the speaker had talked about an historian, the only historian we know of who was writing at the time of Jesus, and recorded Jesus as an historical figure. And the historian referred to Jesus as a hunchback. This news shook Paul Brand's aunt badly. Brand himself was less upset. He remarked that because there was a great deal of TB of the spine in those days it was quite possible that Jesus' back wasn't quite straight. And he said, "I don't mind. I really don't mind." Well, I don't, either.

Among the early church fathers were those who talked of Jesus as being small, frail, long-faced, with eyebrows that joined, dark-skinned, a beautiful and ugly hunchback. In the apocryphal *The Acts of John* is this passage:

"What does this youth want of us? Why is he calling us from the shore?" said my brother James to me.

I said, "My brother James, your eyes must be dimmed by the many sleepless nights we have spent on the lake. Do you not see that the man standing on the shore is a tall man with a joyful face of great beauty?"

My brother said, "I do not see him like that. But let us row ashore and we shall see."

When we hauled up the boat, Jesus himself helped us to make it fast. When we left the place to follow him, he appeared to me as a bald man with a thick-growing beard while to my brother James he seemed a youth with but a faint down on his cheeks, and we could not understand and were amazed.

And so it often happened, and he would appear in forms even more marvelous, sometimes small of stature with crooked limbs, sometimes as a giant reaching for the heavens.

Perhaps he appears to each of us according to our need and according to what God wants of us. We are not to get stuck with any one image, no matter how dear.

If you will notice, the great novelists describe their secondary characters in far more detail than their protagonists. One reason for this is that if the protagonist is not too closely described, it is easier for us to identify with whoever the hero or heroine is—to put ourselves in that person's body.

But another reason is that we see those we love with far more than the outer eye. Think of someone you care about most dearly. Close your eyes and try to visualize that person. It isn't easy, because what we love in someone is far more than just what that person looks like. It is much easier to visualize an acquaintance—someone you do not know with your heart.

So we do not know what Jesus *looked like* any more than we know what those dearest to us *look like*. But we do know what they *are like*. We know them in movement, with their funny little idiosyncrasies that can sometimes irritate us but are basically lovable. We know the *humanness* in them, so that at the very best we know Christ in them. Jesus came to us to call us to be fully human, and Christ is still calling us to that fullness of humanity.

All of the heresies about Jesus Christ come about because we over-emphasize the divinity at the expense of the humanity, or over-emphasize the humanity at the expense of the divinity. Jesus was equally human and divine, and that has always been difficult for us to accept, much less comprehend.

The great hoo-hah about *The Last Temptation of Christ* a while ago came about because of this. I did not see it because I heard it wasn't a very good movie, and Jesus, as usual, was not cast strongly enough. But many of the movie's detractors also had not seen it, and what they were upset about was Jesus' temptations, because these people are (once again) emphasizing his divinity at the expense of his humanity. But we are told that Jesus was tempted in everything, just as we are, but that he did not give in to the temptations.

When Satan tempted Jesus after his baptism, and Jesus rejected the temptations, Satan *left him for a time*. Satan did not let go easily. Immediately after Peter recognized Jesus as the Messiah, the Promised One, Jesus talked of his return to Jerusalem and the trials he must suffer, and Peter protested that this must never happen, and Jesus cried fiercely, *"Get behind me, Satan!"* Of course he did not look forward to the betrayal, the pain, the cross. But he did not give in to the temptation to emphasize his divinity and to forget his humanness.

The more human we become, the more closely we follow Jesus, the less will Satan be able to tempt us.

One of Satan's temptations is *virtue*—making us believe that not only can we be virtuous, but that we can be virtuous by our own merit. And Satan confuses virtue with moralism and legalism. But virtue in Scripture is power, loving power. When the woman with the issue of blood touched the hem of his garment, Jesus felt the *virtue* drain from him.

Satan tempts us to make our virtue a matter of pride. And indeed, pride goes before a fall. Recently we have had several examples of this in Christendom. These people who fell from their pinnacles of virtuous pride were not bad people. They were, on the outside, moral. They tithed, they conducted services, they proclaimed themselves models of what people ought to be, and their very goodness produced pride, and the pride, in some cases, produced a terrible fall. Perhaps if they had preached less about the anger of God and dwelt more on God's forgiveness they would not have done what they did.

Jesus was never proud. He simply *was*. It was the pride of the Pharisees which made Jesus such a threat to them, because he challenged them to let go of their pride and be human. Being human was too frightening—too demanding. And so they tried to trap Jesus.

Recently I read the galleys of a book in which the author rather casually referred to Jesus as a wimp who was into sin, punishment, fear of life, denial of the flesh. Seeing Jesus that way seems to be a human tendency. We are not able to handle the Scriptural character who was robust and open. His first miracle was at a Jewish wedding feast where the guests had already had plenty to drink. But he went ahead and turned water into wine anyhow. Lavishly. And just as lavishly he poured out his own blood for us.

Jesus was lavish in all ways. He loved to laugh, to make jokes. He had a short temper; he occasionally blew his stack. His friends were not "the right people." Most, though not all of them, were from the wrong side of the railroad tracks, and those who belonged to the establishment were often afraid to be seen with him; Nicodemus came to visit him at night, lest he be seen in Jesus' company by his powerful friends at the Sanhedrin. The things that bothered Jesus most in people were hardness of heart, coldness of spirit, self-righteousness, judgmentalness. And he made it very clear that separating people into "us" and "them" was not a good idea. But he did demand that we be human (and remember, to be human does not mean to be perfect; indeed, to be perfect is inhuman). Though we are all called to bear within us the image of God, that image is expressed not through perfection, but through faith, love, passion.

What about the mandate to *be perfect as your Father in heaven is perfect*? The word *perfect* comes from the Latin and means *to do thoroughly*. So, if we understand the word that way, we might say that it means to be human, perfectly human, and perhaps that is what we are meant to understand by this command which is on the surface a contradiction to Jesus' emphasis that only his Father was good, only his Father was perfect. We human beings are to be human—to be perfectly human, not indefectible or impeccable or faultless or superhuman, but complete, right, with integrity undivided. I looked that up in my old thesaurus given me by my father when I was in high school. But no dictionary or thesaurus is going to define humanness for us. The story-teller comes closer.

We tell stories, listen to stories, go to plays, to be amused, to be edified, but mostly so that we can understand what it means to be a human being. Jesus was a story-teller. Indeed, according to Matthew, he taught entirely by telling stories. One of the great triumphs of Satan has been to lead us to believe that "story" isn't true. I don't know if all the facts of the story of Joseph are true, but it is a true story. That is very important to understand. Jesus did not tell his parables in order to give us facts and information, but to show us *truth*. What is the truth of the story of the man with the great plank in his eye? Doesn't it tell us very clearly that we must not judge others more stringently than ourselves?

And Joseph's story tells us much about what it means to be human. More important than whether or not Potiphar's wife actually tried to seduce him is the truth of his integrity in refusing to betray his master. Story is the closest we human beings can come to truth. God is truth. God is beyond the realm of provable fact. We can neither prove nor disprove God. God is for faith.

When I was a child, story helped me find out who I was in a world staggering from the effects of that war which was meant to end war but which, alas, was the beginning of a century of continuing war. Story helped me to accept that human beings do terrible things to other human beings, but that human beings also do marvelous things. Story was a mirror in which I could be helped to find the image of God in myself.

The image of God in ourselves is often obscured, and we surely don't find it in the bathroom mirror. Better mirrors are our friends, those we love and trust most deeply. That image is never found in competition with our neighbours or colleagues; rather, in not wanting to let down those who believe in us and in God's image in us. Each one of us is probably as varied as the Jesus in *The Acts of John*, and which aspect is the more true? Probably the whole bundle together.

Certainly the more human we are, the more varied and contradictory we are. And that is as it should be. God often reveals the infinite Presence to us through paradox and contradiction, and Scripture is full of both. Through paradox and contradiction we are enabled to sift for truth, that truth which will set us free, that truth which is not limited by literalism. What confuses many people about Scripture is that some of it is history, and some of it is story. The story of Joseph may be part history, and part story, but it is *true*.

Is it legalistic literalism which is behind the wave of censorship that is rolling across the land? Are people so afraid of the truth of story that they have to look for some way to deny it? If people look for key words (magic; witch; occult) does that excuse them for disregarding content? In Frances Hodgson Burnett's beautiful book, *The Secret Garden*, the children not only bring a dead garden back to life, but cold hearts are opened in love. Dickon looks at the wonders they have wrought, saying, "It's magic!" and then bursts into song: "Praise God from whom all blessings flow, praise him all creatures here below, praise him above ye heavenly host, praise Father, Son, and Holy Ghost." But because he has used the word *magic* the book is being censored, removed from the shelves as being unChristian. No regard has been paid to content, to what the book *is saying*. The truth underlying the book is beautifully Christian. Censorship is dangerous because there is something inhuman, or mechanical, about it. Jesus couldn't stand inhumanness. Hitler began by burning books and ended by burning people.

However, if I'm upset by the judgmentalism of the extreme Christian right, I'm equally upset at the permissiveness of the more liberal left where, it would seem, almost anything goes. Some of our jargon reflects this. "Lifestyle," for instance, is a word which came into the vocabulary only a decade or so ago, and seems to imply that we can choose any old way of life, as long as we call it our "lifestyle," and that we are permitted—even encouraged—to act out all our feelings, no matter what they are. Believe me, if I acted out all my feelings I'd end in jail.

Relationship is another of my unfavourite overworked, current words. Before it came into the vocabulary we had *friendship* and we had *love*. You can have a relationship without being committed, but not friendship or love. Relationships aren't considered fulfilled unless they end in bed; love involves every part of us, mind and spirit and body, an inseparable trinity. We need to revive friendship and love because these are human emotions. Joseph, being human, refused to have a relationship with Potiphar's wife. Relationships help us avoid being human. But it is our human emotions which help us to face all the joys and sorrows of being human—being betrayed by one's brothers and one's master's wife, being unjustly accused, working through grief, knowing moments of joy, the satisfaction of work well done, the true pleasure of being with friends, of a meal with friends (and Joseph had to eat alone).

Probably my most unfavourite word is *consumer*. How did we ever let the media get away with calling us consumers!? What an ugly noun to use for a human being. Last summer forest fires consumed vast acres of forest. Greedy developers and thoughtless farmers are consuming the great Rain Forests in South America. Drugs consume human beings. So does disease. Consumerism connotes greed, lust, gluttony, avarice, excess, self-centeredness. Can one be a Christian and be a consumer? I doubt it.

Do consumers ever contemplate mortality? I suspect that they shun the thought. But to be human is to be mortal. When Jesus was born in Bethlehem, he was born as all of us are born, to die. He didn't live a long life, but in his three decades he packed all the humanness that any of us need. Of those three decades in Jesus' life we know very little—only the stories of his birth, his visit to the Temple when he was twelve, and the short years of his ministry. But we don't need to know more. The story is there. It is complete. And it shows us the truth about Jesus.

My friend Tallis remarked that the synoptic Gospels, Matthew, Mark, and Luke, are snapshots of Jesus, and that John's gospel is a portrait. Between them they tell us the whole story, and it is a marvelous one.

In the four Gospels it is clear that Jesus was steeped in Hebrew Scripture, in what we call the Old Testament. He quoted from it, referred to it, and expected his hearers to understand it without explanation. We miss much of the New Testament if we are not thoroughly grounded in the Old. For the Old Testament, beginning with Genesis, is the beginning of the story, and we need to understand the beginning in order to understand that there is triumph at the end.

* * *

Asher

We lived simply, but well, we sons of our father. Yes, we all had one father—four mothers, but one father, and though my mother was a concubine, I was as much a son of my father as was Reuben, his first-born. Not as much, however, as Joseph and Benjamin, the favoured two.

Joseph. He was intolerable. I do not miss him. Benjamin is sweet and undemanding and seems not to be aware that our father favours him over the rest of us. He does not brag, nor boast of dreams.

He is the one most at home here in Canaan, for this is all the land he knows as home, whereas the rest of us grew up on our Grandfather Laban's land. But here we are, where our Grandfather Isaac lived and died. Here we are, and have taken wives, sired children, prospered. This land is now our land. El, how I love this land! My land. The mountains bring peace to my soul. The valleys are lush with corn and grapes and grain.

Our wives are sometimes jealous of the fact that we brothers are the sons of our father, that we are together in this land, that we share one God, while they have many. They call on their gods to bring the spring rains, the growing times for fruits and grains, the birth times for the young animals, and for our own children. Perhaps their gods hear.

But now the rains have not come. The sun burns hot with death, not life. We go further and further afield with our flocks to find pasture. The grapes shrivel on the vine. We have grain stored, but it is not enough.

At night the wives leave our tents and join together to sing and dance and call on their goddesses, but in the morning the sun rises again, hot as molten brass. Our father says that we must stop our wives from praying to alien gods. Alien to us, they say, but not to them. And our one God has sent no rain.

The young animals die. We salt down the meat, but it is stringy and tough.

Is God angry with us? Angry that we married wives who have other gods? Is our God not more powerful than those other gods? Did not our God make the stars that shine at night, and the moon that touches our women every month, and the sun that is now brutal in the sky by day? Can he not send rain? We have made sacrifices of our best from the flocks and from the fields. What does El want?

I love my wife and children. My brothers and I work hard. What is wrong? Levi and Simeon scowl. Are we being punished for what they did? Or for what we did, all of us—well, not Reuben, perhaps not Judah, but all the rest of us—to Joseph? We have not told our father that it was not a wild beast who bloodied Joseph's coat. We cannot tell our father.

Can we tell God? Would that make a difference? To say that we sinned, sinned against our own flesh and blood? O God, we have sinned against heaven and before you and are no longer worthy to be called your sons.

Issachar

is a strong ass couching down between the sheepfolds:

And he saw that rest was good, and the land that it was pleasant; and bowed his shoulder to bear, and became a servant under taskwork.

Genesis 49:14-15

Issachar

9

ISSACHAR WAS JACOB'S NINTH SON, Leah's fifth. We know that after the brothers were reconciled, Issachar and his four sons emigrated to Egypt with Jacob's family. But so did Joseph's other brothers. And as with most of them, we know little about Issachar.

It is frustrating to have so little information about Joseph's brothers. We know more about Leah's first sons—Reuben, the compassionate one; Simeon and Levi, who slaughtered Shechem; Judah, who was honest and pragmatic. Of Dan and Naphtali, Gad and Asher, Issachar and Zebulun, our knowledge is scanty. Joseph is the one who engages our attention, whose progress we follow, as he moved through vicissitude and the foibles of fortune into full humanness.

And little Benjamin: even when he is a grown man he is referred to as little Benjamin, the youngest, the baby. When Joseph kept Simeon hostage in Egypt, and sent for Benjamin, the boy would hardly have been a boy any longer, but we still think of him as little Benjamin.

Little Benjamin was rooted in the land of Canaan with his father. Born on the way there, he had never known the land of his grandfather Laban, where the other brothers had been born and grown up. We do well not to worry too much about the chronology of the twelve brothers. The story of Joseph is as much story as history. Jacob thought of little Benjamin as a child, and so should we—little Benjamin, Jacob's last treasure, precious, probably over-protected. His trip to Egypt, at the command of some great, unknown lord in that distant land, was the strangest thing that had ever happened to him.

But for his father, Jacob, it was a terrible wrench, an acute fear that he would lose Benjamin as he had lost Rachel, as he had lost (he thought) Joseph.

Rachel was buried on the way from Laban's land to Isaac's. Jacob knew the place where her bones lay. Fairly frequently in my journal I referred to St. Margaret's graveyard and the bones of my forbears buried there. I wrote, "What does a cemetery mean nowadays? Every once in a while I have a fleeting wish that Hugh was buried over in the Goshen graveyard and that I could go visit the place of his mortal remains. But I don't need a cemetery. His garden is the right place for his ashes; and our life together in Crosswicks, in the apartment in New York, is more than enough of a 'memorial' marker. Every room is full of his presence. I can't believe that our bodies are anything but *gone* when they are gone, and my hope that our soul, our *us*, for want of a better word, is not annihilated, is a hope, not a rigid or legalistic system of belief."

My parents are buried side by side in a graveyard in Florida, not little St. Margaret's graveyard, but a larger one, along with many of my aunts, uncles, cousins, relations, ancestors. One of my cousins, a retired physician, visits the cemetery regularly, and I know that he makes sure that the family plots are properly tended, and I am grateful, for when I go south I do not go to the graveyard. That is not where my parents are. I touch my mother when I put on the piano music she played; when I serve dinner in bowls she used; when I put flowers in her vases. My father is with me when I sit at my desk which was his desk, when I touch his books, when I look at his portrait, painted before I was born, before the war which destroyed his health, a portrait of a vibrant young man in an apple orchard in Brittany, who had just come back from an assignment in Egypt and was wearing a dashing hat he had bought there, and whose eyes are full of life and fun and depth. That portrait is an icon, as my mother's music is an icon.

So we come back again to the question of the soul. Where is Hugh's *Hugh*? I remember looking at my father lying in his coffin when I was seventeen and thinking, "That is not Father. He is not there." And then asking myself—and God—"Where is he?" And believing then, as I do now, deep in my inmost heart, that God still has work for us to do, and the reality of my father, of Hugh, of all that cloud of witnesses, is still real, alive in a way we can't even begin to understand.

But how often God speaks to us in the darkness.

The March after Hugh's death was bleak. I wrote, "It has been a long, cold winter (it is snowing again today), a winter of inner and outer chill. A winter of hard work (too much out-of-town lecturing), revising the book; being grateful beyond words for family and friends. A winter of absences: Hugh's absence; God's absence.

"Then last week came an experience where God's hand was so visible that it was impossible not to recognize it, and out of tragedy came shining affirmation.

"Last Friday I was scheduled to take the shuttle to Boston to speak at Simmons College Friday night and Saturday morning. I planned to spend Saturday afternoon with Danna."

Danna was a young friend who had cancer. She had come through a double mastectomy and chemotherapy with shining faith. She lived near Boston and was a member of a prayer group that was very dear to me, young women, all of the age to have children still at home, who met together to pray, and who had avoided the many pitfalls to which prayer groups are prone.

One of Danna's amusing but apt suggestions was that all prayer groups should read John Updike's *The Witches of Eastwick*. A creative idea. That book certainly points out the pitfalls of spiritual pride!

Danna and I wrote regularly. In one letter she quoted Woody Allen. I can't remember the exact quote, but it was something like, "Life is full of anxiety, trouble, and misery, and it is over too soon." She added, "I love Woody."

In the early autumn she learned that her cancer, which was thought to be cured, had metastasized to the liver. We all knew that things were not good, but it looked as though she might have a year or so more of full living.

So I planned, after my Saturday morning talk, to spend the afternoon with Danna, and then I was to stay over to preach on Sunday morning and take the shuttle home. I was staying with Ethel and Paul Heins, who for so many years were, one after the other, editors of Horn Book, and friends of children's literature and its writers.

On Wednesday I got a call saying that Danna's condition had deteriorated, and she was in Massachusetts General Hospital, but was still looking forward to Saturday afternoon.

On Thursday at two in the afternoon I got a call saying that Danna's blood pressure was dropping rapidly and could I come. *Now.*

I walked home, stuffed a few clothes in an overnight bag, and somehow managed to catch the 3:30 shuttle. I was met by one of the prayer group and her husband and taken directly to the hospital, where I was able to be with Danna and her husband and eldest son, and the members of the prayer group, all of whom were there, caring, praying, and all of whom mentioned God's amazing timing in having me scheduled to be in Boston just at this time.

Ethel and Paul were gracious and kind about having me arrive a day early—and concerned about the reason. It had been planned that Danna's son would pick me up around ten o'clock Friday morning, but he arrived much earlier, while Ethel and Paul and I were having breakfast and we drove right to the hospital. It was apparent that Danna was dying.

I wrote, "It was, in a powerful way, like living through Hugh's death all over again. But I am grateful indeed to have been privileged to have been with Danna as she left this world, and to be with her husband and son.

"I did the jobs at Simmons, preached on Sunday, and stayed to preach at Danna's funeral on Monday. The timing was so incredible that it is impossible to put it down to coincidence. Suddenly, in death and tragedy, God was revealed.

"Danna was a person with a shining spirit, a deep gift of prayer, a merry, bubbling laugh. It is somehow right and proper that God should have chosen her dying as a vessel to reveal the love of the Maker to us all."

Timing. We all saw God's hand in the timing of my trip to Boston. Months later I wrote in my journal: "Each time I write the date I am aware of the passage of time, swift as white water. Time in which strange and irrational things happen, like the deaths of Danna, Gloria, Jean. Cynth had a timely death." I had just come from the memorial for a beloved ninety-two-year-old cousin. "The house in West Price Street (in Philadelphia) is full of memories. I wrote large chunks of *The Small Rain* sitting in the downstairs window seat. Before Hugh and I were married I could always call, 'Is it all right if I come down for a while?' I left Touché [my dog] there while I went to be with Hugh in Washington. Sleeping in 'the little room' where I have so often slept was poignant. Up early, and off to the airport. And here I am in San Antonio.

"The time in each day is precious and precarious. No one knows when some accident will shatter time, some tornado, or heart attack, or gunshot. Perhaps that is why music is so necessary, with its ordered building and structuring of time, and even when there are dissonances or odd chromatics or modulations, they emphasize the exquisite ordering of time.

"Cynth had twenty-two years more than Hugh did. Hugh had twenty years more than Danna or Jean, and well over a decade more than Gloria. How many people get ninety plus years of time that is rich and full of quality as Cynth did? Yes, we can truly say that it is quality and not duration of time that matters—and yet untimeliness is a warping of the music, or a violin string breaking in the midst of playing.

"I had expected that going back to the house on Price Street, so full of memories, that Jean's untimely death might send another wave of grief breaking over me. But no wild sobs have come, no torrent of tears, only a few dry little grunts and groans as I am getting ready for bed. Maybe it's that the emotions of a year ago are too intense, that they would let loose a storm, a rushing waterfall too violent to be poured through the fragile body. I am very carefully not remembering exactly what was happening a year ago today. Something deep in my body is doing the remembering that is too painful for my conscious mind."

A friend struggling with depression said to me, "I just want things to be normal." And I thought: What is normal? Normal is the reality of living with precariousness, of never knowing what is around the corner, when accident or death are going to strike. Normal is cooking dinner for friends in the midst of this precariousness, lighting the candles, laughing, being together. Normal is trusting that God will make meaning out of everything that happens.

So Jacob had to let Benjamin go.

He took the boy in his arms, holding him so tightly that the boy thought his ribs would break, and it was a long time before he understood that his father was weeping for Joseph, the brother who had so long ago been killed by some wild beast. The older brothers had brought home his bright coat stained dark with blood.

They had lived well in Canaan. Jacob's tents were large and comfortable. His flocks and herds had increased. The older brothers were married; their tents with their wives and children stood nearby. They were not prepared for the failure of the crops, for animals dying from hunger and thirst because the pasture land was brown and sere and wells were running dry. Benjamin had never been hungry before.

The corn the brothers had brought back with them from Egypt was soon gone. Jacob instructed his sons to return to Egypt to buy more. But there was one condition, Judah protested—they had been told that the lord of the land would not even see them unless they brought Benjamin. "We must take Benjamin, but I will be surety for him," Judah promised.

So, weeping, Jacob sent them off, bearing gifts (bribes) for the great man in Egypt.

What a strange adventure for Benjamin—his first time away from the home tents, not quite sure what had happened to his brothers in Egypt, or why they had been accused of being spies, or why Simeon was jailed there, or what the money in the bags was all about, or why the great man wanted to see him. But the anxiety of his brothers was palpable.

To leave home, to go into the unknown, is a kind of death. Did Benjamin know that? Are all these other little deaths in life preparation for the death of the body?

Joseph was not yet through playing cat and mouse with his brothers. Was it merely revenge, to pay them back for their betrayal of him? Or was Joseph, too, unsettled and disturbed, seeing his brothers unexpectedly after all these years? Did he, remembering his dreams of the stalks of corn bowing down before him, find the fulfilling of these dreams irresistible?

Cat and mouse. While Hugh was dying, while one thing went wrong after another, to the consternation of his doctors, it seemed that some malign power was playing cat and mouse. Cat and mouse all over the planet. Terrorist attacks in Paris. Strange, deranged men stalking and killing young women. A horrible fire in a South African gold mine—a terrible disaster in an already beleaguered country. We seem to be surrounded by a horror and a hissing and an everlasting reproach.

What is that *normal* my friend was looking for?

The powers of darkness are at work. Another word for them is *echthroi*, Greek for "the enemy," and the echthroi, too, are fighting the light.

Lady Julian of Norwich wrote,

He said not, "Thou shalt not be troubled, thou shalt not be travailed, thou shalt not be distressed," but he said, "Thou shalt not be overcome." It is God's will that we take heed to these words, that we may be ever mighty in faithful trust in weal and woe.

How were Benjamin's brothers to be faithful, taking the youngest away from their father, to a strange lord who had already shown himself to be erratic and unpredictable? As soon as the brothers arrived they were taken to Joseph's house, and again they were terrified. Benjamin was dazzled with what seemed to him to be a palace. His brothers were again speaking all at once, explaining that they had returned the money they had found in their sacks.

And Joseph's chief steward said, *"Peace be to you. Fear not,"* speaking in the familiar words of angels all through the Bible, *"Fear not!"* He went on, *"Your God, and the God of your father, has given you treasure in your sacks." And then he brought Simeon out to them.*

Then they were given water, and their feet were washed (prefiguring Jesus' washing of his friends' feet), *and their animals were given provender.*

When Joseph came home, the brothers gave him the presents they had brought, and bowed themselves to the earth before him. How many of them remembered Joseph's dream, and that this was the fulfillment of it?

Joseph asked them how they were. Then he questioned, "Is your father well, the old man of whom you spoke? Is he still alive?"

And they answered, "Your servant, our father, is in good health. He is yet alive." And they bowed down their heads and made obeisance.

And Joseph lifted up his eyes and saw his brother Benjamin, his mother's son, and said, "Is this your younger brother, of whom you spoke?" And he said to Benjamin, "God be gracious to you, my son."

Joseph was overcome with emotion and left them, because he ached to embrace his brother; so he went into his chamber and wept there. Then he washed his face and controlled himself, and the meal was brought in.

Joseph was served by himself, and the brothers were served by themselves, and Asenath, Joseph's wife, was served by herself, *because the Egyptians might not eat bread with the Hebrews, for that is an abomination unto the Egyptians.*

And later it became an abomination for the orthodox Jew to eat with the unorthodox.

How strange human customs are! When my daughter, Josephine, and her husband, Alan, an Episcopal priest, visited acquaintances in Israel, they were served food and drink, but their host and hostess would not eat with them, because that would have been an abomination to these orthodox Jews!

In my church, the Episcopal Church, it is only in recent decades that God's table has been opened to people of other denominations. And half a century ago a convicted murderer could confess, repent, and then be welcome at the altar rail, but a divorced person could not. In many places we still hold to the kind of division into differing denominations that my Baptist mother-in-law grew up with.

Not long ago I talked with a friend and he told me about reading a Metropolitan Opera bulletin and checking the names of all the singers he knew to be Christians. His question was not, Are they good singers, serving their art to the best of their ability? but, Are they *Christian*? And as we ate at a table with a group of people there was a conversation about whether or not a certain doctor was a Christian—not was he a good doctor, but was he a Christian? Isn't this reversed way of looking at things the reason that so much Christian art isn't very good art? That if you're a Christian that is all that matters? Christian or no, if you are a pianist you have to practise eight hours a day or you won't be a good pianist—or a good Christian. We are not very rational, we human beings who are called to observe and contemplate, but who often get wound up in customs and laws and dogmas and are blinded to that which we are supposed to see.

And Asenath, too, ate alone.

Asenath

And who is the God of the gods?

Is there a God who orders the gods, chastises them for their jealousies and their outrageous demands?

My husband would say that his one god is this god, but his god, too, has limits—is the god of the Hebrew people only. Does he not care for all the rest of us, whether we live or die? This god my husband obeys does not hear the cry of anguish of the Egyptian mother whose child is caught by the crocodile. Only his own people matter to him.

So, he, too, is a god among many gods.

Is there a God whose mercy is over all?

I did not think these thoughts until I was given by my father, Potiphera, to be Joseph's wife. My father is priest of On, and his god is Ra, the sun god. My father is high priest, and has served Ra all his life, Ra who gives both life and death. It was a strange thing to me that I was given to the Hebrew, and it was a mark of how highly the Pharaoh regarded this strange man.

At night we lie together, we know each other. We have our sons, and what must they think about all these strange gods, each one more important (in someone's eyes) than another? There are many gods in Egypt, many priests who serve them, but Ra is the sun. Without Ra it would be perpetual night. Without Ra the Nile would not know when to flood and fertilize the land.

What did it mean to my father, the high priest, to give me to a man whose god was not his god?

My husband is a good man. He is fair. He is just. But he is seldom merry. Sometimes he has laughed when he has played with our sons, tossing them in the air, delighting to hear them shriek with pleasure, knowing themselves safe in his strong arms. With me he is always courteous. At night, when Ra has turned away, my husband brings up from me strange depths of delight, and I please him, too. This I know by his sighs of fulfillment, by his arms that remain around me as he falls into a deep sleep of contentment.

Do our gods know each other? Are they friends? In the darkness when Ra is behind the earth does he laugh with Joseph's god at our lack of understanding? It is not just Ra—this god of Joseph's whose name is unwritten, unspoken, and unpronounceable. In Egypt we have many gods, gods of the underworld, gods to lead us in this life and to lead us in the afterlife. Vultures and crocodiles and the strange black dog, Anubis. A jackal, some say. And there are the goddesses, too, of fertility, fertility for the crops, and for the people, too. Too many gods.

But it was a strong and strange thing for me to be given to Joseph—the Hebrew, the one with the most alien of gods—a tribute to his power, to his ability to rule with justice and not with pride. One might suppose he would have been a threat to the Pharaoh, but he was not. He did what needed to be done and at the end of the day came quietly home to play with our sons, to eat alone, to sleep with me.

Zebulun

shall dwell at the haven of the sea; and he
shall be for an haven of ships; and his bor-
der shall be by Zidon.

Genesis 49:13

Zebulun
10

ZEBULUN WAS THE HEAD of the tenth tribe of Israel. His inherited land was mountainous, but within it was Gath Hepher, where Jonah came from, and Nazareth, Jesus' "home town."

Isaiah writes, *Nevertheless there will be no more gloom for those who were in distress. In the past he humbled the land of Zebulun and the land of Naphtali, but in the future he will honor Galilee of the Gentiles, by way of the sea, along the Jordan.*

And then follow some of Isaiah's most beautiful verses, *The people walking in darkness have seen a great light, on those living in the land of the shadow of death a light has dawned.* And Matthew quotes Isaiah in the fourth chapter of his Gospel: *Leaving Nazareth, he [Jesus] went and lived in Capernaum, which was by the lake in the area of Zebulun and Naphtali, to fulfill what was said through the prophet Isaiah,*

> *"Land of Zebulun and land of Naphtali,*
> *the way to the sea, along the Jordan,*

185

Galilee of the Gentiles—
the people living in darkness
have seen a great light;
on those living in the land of the
shadow of death
a light has dawned."

The Old Testament so often nourishes and informs the New.

Zebulun, meanwhile, came with the brothers from Canaan, to Egypt, to the great lord's palace, was reunited with Simeon, and when they were seated in order of age—Reuben first, then Simeon, and on down to Benjamin—they looked at each other in wonder.

And Joseph put food before them, but Benjamin got five times as much food as any of the others. They ate and were merry with him.

Did Benjamin wonder at this favouritism, or was he used to it? Did it, perhaps, embarrass him? But he was the youngest, so he did not speak. How strange it must have been for Benjamin, receiving special and inexplicable favours from the great lord of Egypt. How strange was Egypt itself, with its buildings of stone, rather than tents of skins, with its huge palaces and temples and tombs—edifices that were built to last forever.

How strange the Pharaonic Egyptian language, into which the brothers' words were translated for the great lord. And how overwhelming for Joseph, to hear them murmuring in his own familiar language, and yet to have to wait to respond until the interpreter gave him the words in Egyptian.

Words have incredible power to heal or to harm. The Name of Jesus is a word of love, and one which I hear misused daily, thoughtlessly, with no evil intent, but weakened and debased by misuse. Words of prayer can be words of healing. It frightens me very much to know that people, not only those in "primitive" tribes, but even people who call themselves Christian, can pray *against* other people. But prayer that is not for love is not truly prayer.

In Joseph's story we note over and over again the power of words. Joseph abuses words by bragging, and pays for his abuse. His brothers use words with murderous intent, and are kept from acting out those words only by Reuben and Judah. Potiphar's wife uses words of false accusation against Joseph, so that he is cast into prison. Malicious gossip can cause terrible harm. Casual, thoughtless words, too, can cause grave damage. More than once it has come to my ears that someone has reported, "Madeleine said . . ." something that Madeleine never said or even thought at all, but the damage has been done.

How powerful words are, and how we seem to forget that power today, with our radical loss of vocabulary. I was horrified to read that the textbook publishing houses are having to simplify the language of the college textbooks because today these books are too difficult for college students, who had no difficulty with them a few decades ago.

As our vocabulary dwindles, so does our ability to think, and so does our theology, and what is theology but the word about God?

Would we quarrel so much about God if we were able to think more clearly about our Maker? I worry about what we are doing to the story God has told about Elself in the greatest story ever told, that of Jesus of Nazareth.

It is easier to see what we are doing to our story in the credal churches, such as my own, where, after great committee effort and expense we have come up with a new

Book of Common Prayer. Now I don't want to go back to the 1928 *Prayer Book*. We needed to think about what we believe in terms of the disturbed twentieth century in which we are living. But we haven't done well by language, and when we do not do well by language, we do not do well by our faith. What distresses me most acutely is that we have changed our story, that greatest story ever told, and without so much as a "by your leave." It is a strange, powerful, difficult story, but it has been our story for nearly two thousand years. If we are going to change it, we should at the very least call a Council of Houston or Omaha or Chicago and do it publicly.

My dearest friend, who is an Episcopalian, senior warden of her church, said to me, "I can't say the creed anymore."

I asked her, "Have you noticed that the language has been changed on you?"

"No."

"Well, it has."

Radically changed. I can't say it anymore, either. In the language of the media I don't believe a word of it. God is a greater story-teller than our recent committees, and we need to reflect back the glory with the greatest language of which we are capable.

I believe in One God, the Father almighty, maker of heaven and earth, and in all things visible and invisible.

Visible and invisible has been replaced with *seen and unseen*, and that's not the same thing at all. If I close my eyes I can't physically see the page in front of me, but it's still visible. I love the idea of the great invisible world that we cannot see, but God can—the world of sub-atomic particles, the world of the galaxies beyond the reach of our greatest telescopes.

Well, it gets worse. We've taken out *Begotten of his Father before all worlds*. That's a terrible omission, because it allows people to forget that Christ was, *was* before the beginning, *was* the Power that shouted all things into being, *was* incarnate for us, and still *is*.

Oh, and even worse. We used to say, *And was incarnate BY the Holy Ghost of the Virgin Mary*. Or, *who was conceived BY the Holy Ghost*. Oh, yes, that's the story, the greatest story ever told. But now we say, weakly, *by the power of the Holy Spirit*. We were all conceived by the power of the Holy Spirit. I was. My babies were. That's the Trinity, shining forth in love: two human beings and the Holy Spirit, and the miracle of a baby. But Jesus was conceived BY the Holy Spirit, and that's a very different story. That's what we used to say.

I have never been particularly hung up over the Virgin Birth. It hasn't been the focus of my faith one way or another. But it has been a significant part of our story and what it truly means is that Jesus' humanity came from his mother, Mary, and that his divinity came from his father, who is God the Holy Spirit. Take away the Virgin Birth and you take away Jesus' divinity.

And now the Virgin Birth has vanished into the lost world of the visible and the invisible. No one has even had the courtesy to ask those of us who go faithfully to church every Sunday, "Do you mind?" I mind.

I mind very much indeed. I can't say the creed in the new, impoverished language either. I don't believe that God is sitting on a golden throne with Jesus at his right hand on a smaller throne. I believe the creed in the language of high poetry, that is, the language of truth, not the language of fact. I think we need to do something about this, not to go backwards, but to admit humbly to ourselves that we have served language poorly, which means serving God poorly. Perhaps the men—they were men, weren't they?—who wrote the new version of the Creed didn't mean to change the story, didn't even know they were changing the story, but that is what, in fact, they did.

The story that got changed is a wonderful story. My friend, Canon Tallis, said that the Virgin Birth was embarrassing to the early Christians. They wouldn't have kept it in if it hadn't happened. God came to us through the womb of a fourteen-year-old girl who had the courage to say to the angel, *"Be it unto me according to your word."*

And what about the angel? What do Scriptural angels say when they come to anyone? *"Fear not!"* That gives us a clue about what angels look like—that the first thing they have to cry out to us is, *"Fear not!"* We've prettied up angels; no longer are they seen as flaming fires, and that's a weakening, too.

The Christian belief is that Jesus was wholly human and Jesus was wholly God. His humanness is his birthing by a young girl, so that Jesus was born as all of us are born. His Godness is that his father is God Elself. That is how the paradox that Jesus is wholly human and Jesus is wholly God is reconciled. If the Virgin Birth is taken away, isn't Jesus' Godness taken away, too?

I sense a kind of limiting chauvinism here. Did the men doing the translation feel that Mary couldn't have done it without one of them—Joseph, or whoever? Jesus was conceived *by* the Holy Spirit—condescending in total love. That is an extraordinary story, and when it got taken away from me, I found that I believe it passionately.

"And it came to pass." "Once upon a time." Wonderful words! To be a human being is to be able to listen to a story, to tell a story, and to know that story is the most perfect vehicle of truth available to the human being. What is so remarkable about the stories of ancient cultures is not their radical diversity, but their unity. We tell basically the same story in all parts of the world, over and over again in varying ways, but it is always the same story, of a universe created by God. We can tell more about God through the words of a story than through any amount of theology.

Joseph was forced to look low for the Creator, dumped into a pit, sold to strangers, sold again in Egypt, thrown into prison, catapulted into power. And with each strange reversal he grew, grew into a human being. To grow into a human being is not to grow into *humanism*, for humanists believe only in man, able to do it on his own without the help of God. To be a human being is to know clearly that anything good we do is sheer gift of grace, that God's image in us shines so brightly that its light is visible.

While Joseph's brothers ate the feast prepared for them he looked at them, his heart full, but he was not yet ready to reveal himself to them, and so he could not touch them. Men were not afraid to touch each other in those days, to fling their arms around each other in hilarity or grief or forgiveness, and Joseph must have longed particularly to touch Benjamin, his full brother, now grown to a comely young man.

After the brothers had eaten, Joseph ordered their bags to be filled with corn, and they bade him farewell with much gratitude, if considerable perplexity, and set off for Canaan. This time Simeon was with them and their hearts were light.

But then again they were faced with the unexpected, and further terror. The cat was not through playing with the mice. Was that all it was for Joseph? Mere cat play? Or was there anguish in his heart, too? We human beings are often unaware of our deepest motives, and our motives, at their best, are usually mixed. Joseph was settled in Egypt, in a position of power—power that involved incredibly hard work, but still power. He was married to Asenath. He had sons. He had put Canaan and his family behind him, perforce. His brothers had betrayed him with "a horror and a hissing and an everlasting reproach." There was no point in looking back. He had to make his home in Egypt, to live as a stranger in a strange land.

Now he sent his steward riding after his brothers, and the steward stopped them and accused them of taking his master's silver cup.

They were horrified.

"No, no!" Reuben cried. *"How can you say such things to us? Why would we take your lord's silver cup after his great kindness to us?"*

All the brothers protested their innocence loudly, and Reuben continued, *"You know that the money which we found in our sacks we brought again to you from the land of Canaan. How, then, should we steal silver or gold out of your lord's house? If any among us has anything of your master's, he will surely die."*

All the bags were opened. And there, in Benjamin's sack of grain, the silver cup was found.

The brothers looked at each other, and at Benjamin. There was terror in their eyes, in their voices.

Wordlessly, Reuben picked Benjamin up and helped him onto his donkey, and the brothers turned back towards Egypt.

Benjamin was silent, terrified. Reuben had said that whoever took the silver cup would surely die, and Benjamin felt a great weight of horror. He had not taken the cup; why was it in his bag? Why? Why did the great lord heap his plate with more food than any of the brothers? What did he want?

It was a heavy and silent ride back to Joseph's palace, where he was waiting for them. He confronted them, *"What deed is this that you have done? Did you not know that a man such as I am can certainly divine?"*

And Judah said, hopelessly, *"What shall we say to my lord? What shall we speak? God has found out the iniquity of your servants. Behold, we are my lord's servants, both we, and he also with whom the cup is found."* Judah's dark eyes were bleak. It was apparent to Benjamin that this older brother believed that they were all going to be killed for this thing that not one of them had done.

Joseph looked at Benjamin, and his eyes were surprisingly mild. He told them that the one in whose sack the cup was found would be his servant. Then he said to the others, *"As for you, get you up in peace to your father."*

In peace, without Benjamin?

Judah approached Joseph and said, *"Oh, my lord, let your servant speak a word in my lord's ears, and let not your anger burn against your servant."* And he pleaded with Joseph not to take Benjamin away from his father.

"Do not be angry with your servant, though you are equal to Pharaoh himself. My lord has asked his servants if we have a father or a brother. And we answered, 'We have an aged father, and there is a young son born to him in his old age. His brother is dead, and he is the only one of his mother's sons left, and his father loves him.' After we had told you this, my lord told your servants to bring our young brother to him, and we said to my lord that we could not take our brother away from our father, for if we did so, our father would die. But you told your servants that unless we brought our youngest brother to you we would never see Simeon again." And so he went on, an impas-

sioned speech, a brave speech, because Judah had to acknowledge openly that the sons of Rachel were more dear to their father than the sons of the other wives. Judah ended by crying, *"If the boy is not with us when we go back to our father, and if our father, whose life is closely bound up with the boy's life, sees that we do not have the boy with us, he will die. Your servants will bring the grey head of our father down to the grave in sorrow. Your servant guaranteed the boy's safety to our father. I said, 'If I do not bring him back to you, I will bear the blame before you, my father, all my life.' Now then, please let your servant remain here as my lord's slave in place of the boy, and let the boy return with his brothers. How can I go back to my father if the boy is not with me? No! Do not let me see the misery that would come upon my father!"*

At these words of anguish Joseph could no longer control himself in front of all his attendants, and, interrupting the interpreter he cried out, "Go away!" His servants and attendants looked at him wonderingly.

"Leave me!"

And they left him. At last he was alone with his brothers.

∗ ∗ ∗

Benjamin

"Go away!" the great man orders all his servants. He heaves with sobs like a child, and all his retinue hurry to leave him. My brothers and I are frozen. Rooted to the spot. We cannot move.

And the great man weeps, and then he lifts me in his arms as though I were a small child—how strong he is!—and then he cries out, *"I am Joseph! And does my father yet live?"*

And no one dares answer him. They are all still afraid. But he holds me as once my sister Dinah held me, and I put my arms about his neck as though I were still a child, and I say, "Yes. Our father lives."

And now I know why he seemed familiar to me: he is my one full brother, my mother's son.

"And our mother," I breathe, "do you remember our mother?"

He holds me even more closely. "Yes. I remember our mother." And he tells me about her, how beautiful she was, and always sweet-smelling. In a land of tents made of skins, and of dust, and camel dung, always she smelled sweet. And when she knew that she was with child, with me, how happy she was, and how happy he was, too, and our father—and then, in birthing me, she died.

And again he wept, and I wept, too, for the mother I had never known. Oh, I wasn't lonely, and I wasn't unmothered. I had, you might say, mothers to spare. Too many mothers. But I was loved; I did not lack for love. And yet I wept, for loss of my mother, for gain of my brother.

And our brothers stood and their eyes were full of sorrow and full of anxiety.

"Come near to me," Joseph said to our brothers, and slowly, one by one, they came near. And he said, *"I am Joseph, your brother, whom you sold into Egypt."*

And they bowed their heads, and their eyes were downcast and they mumbled.

And Joseph said, speaking kindly, his arm still about me as I stood beside him, *"Do not be grieved, or angry with yourselves, that you sold me, because God sent me before you to preserve life. You meant it for evil, but Yahweh meant it for good."*

God's plan. Did God send Joseph to Egypt? If my brother had stayed in Canaan, he would not have saved the corn and grain to avert famine.

Was my mother's death part of God's plan? Was there some good purpose that it served that I do not yet know about?

Joseph told us that the famine would continue for five more years. And he said, *"God sent me before you to preserve you a posterity in the earth, and to save your lives by a great deliverance. So it was not you who sold me into Egypt, but God, and he has made me a father to Pharaoh and lord of all his house, and ruler throughout all the land of Egypt."*

"Sold into Egypt? Who sold someone into Egypt?" I ask.

Joseph turns away. Simeon and Levi turn away. The others stare down at their feet, those feet washed by Joseph's servants after the dirty and dusty trip from Canaan. No one speaks.

I ask again.

Reuben and Judah draw me aside. Try to explain. Neither one tries to clear himself, but each one says that it was the other who did not want Joseph killed.

Killed.

My brother killed by his own brothers. My heart beats with new fear.

Only Reuben and Judah had held back from killing. Reuben wanted to rescue Joseph from the pit and bring him back to our father. But the others—and Judah did not stop them—sold him to a group of traveling merchants on their way to Egypt.

How can I ever feel safe with my brothers again?

What will our father—

But Joseph turns then and comes to me and tells me I must never, ever, say anything to our father. It would kill him, Joseph says, and Reuben and Judah nod agreement.

I am made to promise.

So I do. What purpose would it serve to grieve our father, when we can bring him such joy? And how he will rejoice that Joseph is alive!

I think again about what Joseph said about God's plan.

"Do you truly think it was God's plan for our brothers to sell you into Egypt?" I demand.

He nods.

"I do not understand."

"You do not need to understand," Joseph says gravely. "Nor do I. I only know that where there was great hurt, there is now great good, and that our God can come into all our pain and make use of it, as he has done with me." And he opens wide his arms to all the brothers, all of them.

And there are tears. And there is joy.

Joseph

is a fruitful bough, even a fruitful bough by a well, whose branches run over the wall:

The archers have sorely grieved him, and shot at him, and persecuted him: But his bow abode in strength, and the arms of his hands were made strong by the hands of the mighty God of Jacob;

Even by the God of thy father, who shall help thee; and by the Almighty, who shall bless thee with blessings of heaven above, blessings of the deep that lieth under, blessings of the breasts, and of the womb:

The blessings of thy father have prevailed above the blessings of my progenitors unto the utmost bound of the everlasting hills: they shall be on the head of Joseph, and on the crown of the head of him that was separate from his brethren.

Genesis 49:22-26

Joseph
11

OF COURSE Benjamin would not have known of his brothers' treachery, and his reaction would have awakened Joseph's pain. Pain, lying long dormant, can rise up and be as acute as when it was first felt. The wonderful letters I have received since the publication of *Two-Part Invention: The Story of a Marriage* have reawakened my pain at Hugh's illness and death. The letters speak affirmation and joy; yet grief that had been drowsing, if not sleeping, is suddenly wide awake.

We don't "get over" the deepest pains of life, nor should we. "Are you over it?" is a question that cannot be asked by someone who has been through "it," whatever "it" is. It is an anxious question, an asking for reassurance that cannot be given. During an average lifetime there are many pains, many griefs to be borne. We don't "get over" them; we learn to live with them, to go on growing and deepening, and understanding, as Joseph understood, that God can come into all our pain and make something creative out of it.

Through his pain Joseph had learned to be a human being. And he had learned that to be human is to be fallible, and therefore in the end he harboured no hate nor held a grudge against his brothers.

To be human is, yes, to be fallible. We are the creatures who *know*, and we know that we know. We are also the creatures who know that we don't know. When I was a child, I used to think that being grown up meant that you would know. Grown-ups had the answers. This is an illusion that a lot of people don't lose when they grow up. But our very fallibility is one of our human glories. If we are fallible we are free to grow and develop. If we are infallible we are rigid, stuck in one position, as immobile as those who could not let go the idea that planet earth is the centre of all things.

I was talking about this to a friend, and she said, "You don't think the pope is infallible?" And I laughed, because that wasn't what I was thinking at all. The pope is the pope. The Church has always tended to make absolute statements, and absolutism has always caused trouble. It was absolutism that caused the disastrous split between the Eastern and Western Churches, which was the beginning of the continuous and devastating fragmentation of Christendom.

When I was speaking at a Mennonite college I was told that the split between the Mennonites and the Amish in the seventeenth century came about because of buttons. *Buttons*. One group, I forget which, decided it was all right to wear buttons because they were useful. The other said, no, buttons are a decoration and are sinful. And they split over buttons.

Peripheral. And each fragment of the church, from the extreme evangelical right to the extreme permissive liberal left is convinced of the Bible's infallibility or the pope's infallibility or the infallibility of the creeds or the infallibility of not having creeds.

Wait! Did I imply that Scripture is not infallible? Scripture is true, and fallibility and infallibility is not what Scripture is about. According to Scripture it is perfectly all right to have slaves as long as you treat them kindly. Slaves are told to be diligent and loyal to their masters. The psalmist says that he never saw the good man go hungry or his children begging for bread. Yet we know that good men do go hungry and their children do beg for bread every day. In his letter to the people of Thessalonica Paul's harsh words about the Jews have encouraged the ugliness of anti-Semitism: *"It was the Jews who killed their own prophets, the Jews who killed the Lord, Jesus, the Jews who drove us out, his messengers."* Taken out of the context in which Paul was writing to the suffering Thessalonians, his words can do untold harm, and they have often done so.

So what do I believe about Scripture? I believe that it is true. What is true is alive and capable of movement and growth. Scripture is full of paradox and contradiction, but it is true, and if we fallible human creatures look regularly and humbly at the great pages and people of Scripture, if we are willing to accept truth rather than rigidly infallible statements, we will be given life, and life more abundantly. And we, like Joseph, will make progress towards becoming human.

There are some creatures which are not given the blessing of fallibility—those insects that live totally by instinct. The instinct of an insect has to be infallible or it will perish. Every ant in an ant colony knows exactly what to do, when to do it, and how to do it. And an ant which deviates from the infallible pattern is a goner.

An ant has superb instincts, but precious little free will. Free will involves fallibility. An ant approached by Potiphar's wife would not have had the free will to say, *No*—or *Yes*.

With free will, we are able to try something new. Maybe it doesn't work, or we make mistakes and learn from them. We try something else. That doesn't work, either. So we try yet something else again. When I study the working processes of the great artists I am awed at the hundreds and hundreds of sketches made before the painter begins to be ready to put anything on the canvas. It gives me fresh courage to know of the massive revision Dostoevsky made of all his books—the hundreds of pages that got written and thrown out before one was kept. A performer must rehearse and rehearse and rehearse, making mistakes, discarding, trying again and again.

One of my favourite stories when I was a child was that of the Scottish leader Robert Bruce and the spider. Bruce had lost yet another battle. He had crawled into a cave, wounded and defeated. He was giving up. And while he lay there he watched a spider spinning her web. To make its perfection complete she had to throw a strand of silk to the center of the web. She threw and missed. Threw and missed. Six times she missed. But the seventh time she threw, the silk flew to its perfect place.

So Robert Bruce left the cave, gathered his people together, and together they fought one more battle. And this time they won.

The memory of that story, read when I was a small child, has stayed with me all these years. I, too, like most of us, have had to throw that strand of silk over and over again.

Infallibility and perfectionism go hand in hand. Perfectionism is a great crippler. We must be willing to try, to make mistakes, to try not to make the same mistakes too often, but to keep on trying. If I were a perfectionist I couldn't get the pleasure I do out of playing the piano, because there isn't any way that I can play like Rubenstein. But I don't have to be perfect. I have to listen to my fingers and hear what I *want* them to do perhaps more than what they are actually doing. But I don't have to be perfect. I just have to enjoy.

Joseph was a great mathematician. He had to be, in order to figure out the complicated logistics of storing food for seven years for the great land of Egypt, of distributing it, not only to the Egyptians, but to those who came from Canaan and other lands, of knowing how much to give and how much to keep in order that the supply might last until the time of famine was over. And, like all great mathematicians, he was an artist. The artist cannot be an artist without believing in the goodness of matter, of all that has been made; the artist cannot be an artist without having faith that what God has created is delightful and to be rejoiced in. Sometimes the man of business can fall into the Manichaean heresy of assuming that only spirit is good and all matter is evil. Is it coincidence that Puritans denigrated the joys of sex but were successful in business? Joseph refused Potiphar's wife's advances because he would not betray his master, but he knew and enjoyed his own wife, Asenath.

Joseph, as a great mathematician, managed to combine a cool business sense with the *art* of numbers, and this combination is what business too often lacks. One of the horrors of the Industrial Revolution was that its factories reduced many of the workers to a state little better than bees in a hive or ants in a hill, and along with this denigration of the value of our humanness came the suspicion of the arts as being a "tool of the devil."

In this very century—not now, but in the early years—an actor could not be buried in consecrated ground. I was married to an actor for forty years, and I know that in his acting he was true, not infallible, but true. Many Christians have either tended to toss the arts off as unreal and unimportant, or as being sinful. And that is to miss the point. Anything good—and all that God made is good—can be distorted and made ugly and bad. That does not change the original good. I am glad that Joseph refused Potiphar's wife, even though it meant his going to jail. I am glad that he enjoyed Asenath.

If we have to be infallible we are not free to seek truth. We are not free to say *No*, this time, and *Yes*, that time. Truth often comes by revelation when we least expect it. It was in the middle of the night that I realized that Benjamin would have no idea that his brothers, his own brothers, had sold Joseph into Egypt.

My writing teaches me. It gives me truths I didn't know and could never have thought of by myself. Truth is given us when we are enabled to believe the contradictory and impossible. Jesus is wholly God? Jesus is wholly human? That's impossible. But it is the conjunction of these two impossibilities that make light.

Stagehands refer to light plugs as female plugs and male plugs. I remember hearing a stagehand yell, "Give me a male plug." You have to have a male plug and a female plug to get light.

Light itself is a particle, and light is a wave. It is not that difficult to believe in the impossible because it is the impossible that gives us joy. The possible really isn't worth bothering about.

One of the bits of dogma that used to concern me was that Jesus is exactly like us—except he's sinless. Well, of course if he's sinless he's not exactly like us; he's not like us at all. And then I arrived at a totally different definition of sin. Sin is not child abuse or rape or murder, terrible those these may be. Sin is separation from God, and Jesus was never separate from the Source. Of course if we were close to our Source, if we were not separated from God, it would be impossible for us to commit child abuse or rape or murder. But when we are separated from God, that sin makes all sins possible.

Far too often we drift away from the Creator even if we don't deliberately turn away. We fall into self-satisfaction or self-indulgence. And we want above all things to be right. To insist on being infallible is to turn away from our Source, for only the Creator is infallible. And whenever we look for infallibility in any one of us, or in ourselves, we are putting ourselves in the place of God. *Hubris*: pride. That, of course, is the great danger of idolatry, of idolizing another human being. We are turning that human being into God, and of course no human being can be God—and disaster follows.

When we are without sin, we are totally in communion with the Creator who made us, along with galaxies, and quasars, and quail eggs, and quarks.

All I have to know is that I do not have to know in limited, finite terms of provable fact that which I believe.

Infallibility has led to schisms in the Church, to atheism, to deep misery. All I have to know is that God is love, and that love will not let us go, not any of us. When I say that I believe in the resurrection of the body, and I do, I am saying what I believe to be true, not literal, but true. Literalism and infallibility go hand in hand, but mercy and truth have kissed each other. To be human is to be fallible, but it is also to be capable of love and to be able to retain that childlike openness which enables us to go bravely into the darkness and towards that life of love and truth which will set us free.

Sometimes when I think about us human beings with all of our quirks, all of our flaws, all of our strangeness, our hilariousness, I wonder why God chose to make us this way. I have to assume that God knows better than I do, that this is indeed the way we are supposed to be, human beings bearing God's image within us. In the same way that we don't *see* those we love, but *know* those we love, we don't *see* God's image, but we *know* God's image. It is not a matter of sight but a matter of insight.

We human beings are creatures who live with questions that lead to new questions. What few answers there are come in the form of paradox and contradiction. I believe in the power of prayer. I believe in miracles, although Spinoza felt that a miracle was a denial of God's existence. Spinoza says,

> Now, as nothing is true save only by Divine decree, it is plain that the universal laws of Nature are decrees of God following from the necessity and perfection of the Divine nature. Hence, any event happening in nature which contravened Nature's universal laws, would necessarily also contravene the Divine decree. . . . Therefore, Miracles, in the sense of events

contrary to the laws of Nature, so far from demonstrating to us the existence of God, would, on the contrary, lead us to doubt it.

Since the universe is God's, I don't see why love can't alter any law which Love demands. Jesus made it very clear that love comes before law. So I have no trouble with miracles. The problem is: Why is *this* miracle granted, and *this* miracle withheld? Why does this child live and this child die? Why is one person cured and not another? Why is this prayer answered with a wonderful *Yes*, and other prayers with silence, or a *No*?

We don't understand the "no" answers, and probably we are not going to understand many of them in this life. But we will understand ultimately that the "no" always has a reason. When we say *No* to our children, we say *No* because there is a reason for saying *No*, a reason for their greater good. When my kids were little I'd say, "Do what I tell you to do when I tell you to do it. *Then* I'll explain to you that there's a truck coming down the road." Quite often we simply do not see the truck on the road that God is warning us against. We may never in this life know that it was about to run us down.

Surely when Joseph was sold into Egypt he knew only the ugliness of what his brothers had done, and had no inkling of how God was going to use it for good.

To be human is to be able to change, knowing full well that some change is good and some change is bad; some change is progressive and some is regressive, and we often cannot discern which is which. But if we lose the ability to change we stultify, we turn to stone, we die.

Remember, yesterday's heresy is tomorrow's dogma. Nowadays even the most avid creationists don't burn those who believe in the possibility of evolution. Giordano Bruno was burned at the stake because he had moved on from the belief that planet earth is the centre of all things to understanding that we are part of a universe—a glorious, exciting part, called on to observe and contemplate, but still only a part.

The Church with its reluctance to change helped, if not forced, scientists into a position of atheism, in which many of them remain stuck to this day, with the absurd idea that religion and science have nothing in common and are, indeed, in conflict. The Church insisted, and sometimes still insists, that if you do not believe in God in a certain, specific, rigid way, then you are not a Christian. And so you come to equal folly on the part of the scientists. An article in the *New York Times* quoted the Academy of Sciences as saying that "religion and science are separate and mutually exclusive realms of human thought." Here is another example of rigidity and short-sightedness. At their best and wisest, religion and science enrich each other.

When Moses asked God his name, God said, "I am. Tell them that I AM sent you. I am that I am." The better, more accurate translation is, "I will be what I will be." Free. Free to manifest the glory in more brilliant ways of revelation than we can conceive of.

All through Scripture, the revelation of God and the people's understanding of God change. In the early chapters there are two quite different ways of looking at God, as there are two Creation stories, and two stories of the forming of Adam and Eve. There was a tribal god, who was one god among many gods. This tribal god was the warrior god of the patriarchs, who would expel the heathen from their own land so that his own people could occupy it, because the heathen were "them" and the tribal god wanted "us" to have the land.

Shattered remnants of this tribal thinking were behind England's empire, and behind our own treatment of the American Indians as we moved into the American continents. This refusal to change in our understanding of the Creator has brought about some very dehumanizing results, one of the least of which was forcing "them" to eat alone.

But there is also in Genesis a vision of the One God, the Maker of the Universe, the stars, and all things. This One God, unlike the tribal god, is a God of love, the One Jesus called Father, Abba, Daddy. There are suggestions in the Old Testament that the tribal god has a bad temper and is likely to throw thunderbolts if we arouse his anger, but the One God, the Creator, is lovingly merciful, quick to forgive. As Alan Jones reminds us, God says, "All is forgiven! Come home!"

We human beings are less quick than God to forgive, and quite a few Old (and New) Testament characters complain about God's forgiveness, saying that it is not reliable of God to be so forgiving, to say, "Come home. Let's have a party. Get out the fatted calf . . ." But God is love, and that love keeps breaking through our elder-brotherism, our stiff-neckedness, our resentments, our unwillingness to change. It is interesting in the story of Joseph and his brothers that Reuben and Judah, two elder brothers, were willing to change.

An amazing number of physicists have discovered that a belief in evolution does not necessarily mean that the Creation of the universe was happenstance. It is quite possible that this is how God *chose* to create. But it is important to remember that our present knowledge is far from the whole truth, and we probably have as far to go as the old earth-centred establishments in understanding the working of the Creator.

John said to the people of Laodicea, *"I know what you are. You are neither hot nor cold. I wish you were hot or cold. But because you are neither hot nor cold but lukewarm I will spew you out of my mouth."*

Let us not be lukewarm. If we are passionate (rather than fanatic) we may be totally wrong (fanatics are never wrong), but we are still capable of change, capable of saying, "I'm wrong. I'm sorry."

Computers are passionless. I can probably have a relationship with my computer, but it is not love. And computers at airports cannot cope with apostrophes, and I'm having a terrible time keeping the apostrophe in L'Engle. I don't plan to give in to the computer and give it up. Computers do not know how to change. But we are able to change because we have passion—or better, *compassion*.

To be willing to change is to be willing to let go our most cherished beliefs, be they religious or scientific. But no scientific discovery has ever shaken my faith in God as Creator and Lover of us all. That is central. The rest—Baptist or Episcopalian, creationist or evolutionist—is peripheral. We are at a time on our planet when we must return to the central things, to understanding that we are all human beings on a very small planet and that we have, as Gandhi said, "enough for everyone's need but not for everyone's greed."

God feels deep pain when any of creation is rebellious and has turned against the Power of Love which made it all. We have hospitals because people cared about taking care of people who were ill or injured. By and large hospitals are not very good right now, but the love that started them was right. It's just that our technological knowledge has grown too fast and our compassion can't keep up

JOSEPH

with it, and a resurgence of compassion is essential. We can't have the absolute magnificent feast until everyone is well, and until everybody—Simeon and Levi, all of the family—is there, until everyone has said, "I'm sorry, I want to come home." And then the golden gates will fling open and the party can start.

When we are in communion with the Creator we are less afraid, less afraid that the wrong people will come to the party, less afraid that we ourselves aren't good enough, less afraid of pain and alienation and death. Jesus, who comes across in the Gospels as extraordinarily strong, begged in the garden, with drops of sweat like blood running down his face, that he might be spared the terrible cup ahead of him, the betrayal and abandonment by his friends, death on the cross. Because Jesus cried out in anguish, we may too. But our fear is less frequent and infinitely less if we are close to the Creator. Jesus, having cried out, then let his fear go, and moved on.

A few months after my husband's death I went to speak at Brigham Young University in Provo, Utah. One of the professors asked me, "What has your husband's death made you think about death?"

I answered, "It's made it seem much less important."

"What do you mean by that?" he asked.

I don't know what I meant by that. I just told him what was. Probably it had something to do with closeness—closeness to the Creator and therefore to all of Creation—past, present, future, not separated by time, but part of God's eternal is-ness.

Eternity is not a time concept. It is almost impossible for us to glimpse what eternity is like because we were born into time. Our bodies move through time. We will die in time. But eternity, that which we are promised, has nothing whatsoever to do with time. It is not time stretched out, on and on forever. It is something wholly different.

My forbears and their contemporaries in St. Margaret's graveyard on Fleming's Island knew during their lifetimes far more about death than we do, because death was far more present. There are not very many old people in that graveyard. There are many children a year, two years, three years old, cut down by diphtheria or scarlet fever. My cousin Myra, my mother's first cousin, told me that when she was a child, five of her brothers and sisters died of scarlet fever in a week. Those who managed to grow up faced malaria, yellow fever, and pneumonia—with no antibiotics. It was not possible to forget or hide death then as secular society today urges us to do. To lose five children in a week! How did the families endure such grief? They endured it because they had to, and such tragedies were not uncommon. Only faith kept the living going.

It is no longer possible—for me, at any rate—to have the same kind of literal faith that my ancestors did. We have acquired a lot of knowledge, as well as antibiotics, since then. Our knowledge has kept people alive today who would have died early deaths a century ago. When there were a few cases of scarlet fever in our village when my children were little my first reaction (remembering Cousin Myra) was panic. I was told to relax; with our new medications, scarlet fever was no longer a killer. A century ago I, myself, would have died twice in childbirth, hemorrhaging, like Rachel, with no way to staunch the blood. Our medical knowledge exploded during and after World War II, and our miracles of science are miracles indeed. But we have saved lives so successfully that we tend to forget that to be human is ultimately to die. Our thinking about death has atrophied to the point where we reject it as being a medical failure. People are put away in hospitals or nursing homes so that we don't have to be tainted by death and perhaps catch it.

We are all going to die, and I suppose whether it is sooner or later makes little difference in eternity, for eternity is total is-ness, immediacy, now-ness. Living in eternity is, in fact, the way we are supposed to live all the time, right now, in the immediate moment, not hanging onto the past, not projecting into the future. The past is the rock that is under our feet, that enables us to push off from it and move into the future. But we don't go bury ourselves in the past, nor should we worry too much about the future. "Sufficient unto the day . . ." my grandmother was fond of quoting. God in Jesus came to be in time with us and to redeem human time for us— human time, wristwatch time *(chronos)*, and God's time *(kairos)*. But even *chronos* is variable. How long is a toothache? How long is a wonderful time? When I fly from New York to San Francisco to see my eldest daughter and her family, I have to set my watch back three hours and I always have jet lag. Even chronological time is full of surprises.

We know that we will never get out of the solar system as long as we have to travel at the speed of anything, even light, because the inter-galactic distances are so enormous. Added to that, the faster a moving body moves, the more slowly time moves. So if we got into a spaceship and went to Alpha Centauri, which is seven light years away, and turned right around and came back, we'd have been away for fourteen years. But about a hundred and fifty years would have passed on earth while we were away. So travel at the speed of anything involves the whole space-time continuum which is still something we do not understand.

In the heart and spirit we are less restricted by time. We are given glimpses of *kairos* in our own living, moments that break free of time and simply are. It is fascinating that music is so bound up with time and yet some of the greatest moments of music are the silences between notes. We all have moments of *kairos*, though we seldom recognize them till afterwards. One such glimpse that I remember with particular delight came after a long and very difficult labour when my doctor and friend dropped a small wet creature between my breasts, saying, "Here's your son, Madeleine." And I heard the angels sing.

It can be far less cosmic. It can be dinner with friends. Last spring when I came home from the hospital after knee surgery, my bed became the dining room table. One evening five young friends brought in dinner, and afterwards were sitting on or around the bed, and we began to sing hymns and folk songs. One of the girls started "Patrick's breastplate," one of the longest hymns I know, and we sang it all, every single verse. And it took a fraction of a second. It is, as always, paradox.

And I rejoice.

I want my church to think about eternity. I want to hear preached from the pulpit the Good News of Christ coming into time for us in order to show us how to be human. I want to hear the affirmation that God is powerful enough to do something with ashes if, indeed, something needs to be done. I want to hear that my husband's soul (yes, let's call it that), and the souls of my parents, my friends, are safe in God's care, reclothed in the "spiritual body," growing in God's love. I want to be helped to understand that we are not always ready to receive God's love, that we turn away with selfishness, permissiveness, despair, but that God is always waiting for our cold hearts to turn warm, our anger to peace, our willfulness to love. When we truly love someone we do not want to let that person down. We want to please, not to get Brownie points, but because we love. I want to love God so much that I will no longer obscure the lovely light, but will let it burn brightly.

It took a long time for Joseph to turn from being spoiled and arrogant to being humble and loving. But that's all right. The promise is not that it will be easy but that it will be wonderful.

✴ ✳ ✶

Joseph's Servant

He is a strange man. Kind to me always. To all of us. There are no floggings in his house. We eat as well as he eats. Better, because we eat together and are merry while he, perforce, eats alone. He has more power than Pharaoh, but he is a Jew. He eats alone.

He is a strange man. In his house we are given an atmosphere for merriment. He likes to hear us laugh, though he seldom smiles. He likes to hear us make music; sometimes he even beats out the time, but he does not sing. He gives us freedom, but, despite his power, he is not free.

Asenath, his wife, is beautiful and loving. Their sons are bright and full of laughter. Are they Egyptians, or are they Jews? They go to the great stone temple with their grandfather, the priest of On. They watch the rising and the setting of the sun and sing the hymns. Sometimes I hear them talk about their father's God as of a distant stranger. Do they know who they are? They are still too young for such questions.

He is a strange man, their father. Always it is as though he is waiting, waiting, but for what? He has everything a man could want. Always it is as though something is missing, but what could it be? He works hard, from sunrise to sunset, overseeing, supervising. He is fair. He cannot be bribed. I know, because when a man with heavy gold earrings and much wealth tried to buy, at a high price, more than his share of corn, I saw my master white with anger. He flung the proffered money at the man's feet, turned on his heel, and went into the counting house.

He is a strange man, attractive to women, though he does not seem to realize it, or, if he does, he will have none of their wiles. It is not unusual for the privileged and powerful to add a beautiful woman or two to their privilege and power. But not my master, Joseph, who each night retires with his wife Asenath to their rooms. We servants are sent away, even the two body servants, that they may be alone.

He is a strange man. When he eats his meals alone, it is as though he is waiting for someone to join him. When he rides his beautiful black mare, it is as though he is looking for someone to ride beside him. He does not speak of what it is that is missing, not even to Asenath, I think. But there is always an unfilled space at his side, even when he plays with his boys.

And now that space is filled with ten strange men from Canaan, men with dark beards half hiding their faces, and with dark eyes, dark as my master's. He speaks to them roughly, as I have never before heard him speak to any of the hungry people coming to Egypt to buy food.

Who are they, that they make him weep? Yet, after all his roughness, he sends them away with their sacks filled with corn and wheat, and, after they are gone, he is restless. He has, for what reason I cannot guess, kept one of these men behind as a prisoner. The man is treated well, given fine clothing to wear, the best of food and wine. But my master does not visit him. He gives orders that the man be treated as an honored guest, and he knows that no one would dream of disobeying. And the man asks no questions. He does not ask why he is being held in a single, though spacious, room, with guards to see that he does not leave. He does not ask why he is given silken garments and delicacies to eat. Why does he not ask? Strange, indeed.

Yes, he, too, with his lack of questions, is a strange man, as my master is strange. My master paces when he is not working, paces, back and forth as though waiting. Sometimes Asenath has to call him three times before he hears. His work goes on. He does not slacken. But he paces.

And then at last the bearded men return, and with them a younger one, and my master prepares a great feast for them, and heaps food on the young lad's plate, and looks at him with hungry eyes. And then, again, I see those great eyes fill with tears, and he shouts at us servants, raising his voice. "Leave us!" he cries. At first we are too terrified to move. "Leave us!" And so we go.

And now the empty space is filled. He waits for unseen guests no longer. For the men from Canaan are his brothers, and now I hear him sing, at last I hear him sing, thanks and praise to his God who makes patterns of the stars in the sky and patterns of the people on earth, and with his patterning has brought twelve brothers together.

Benjamin

is a wolf that raveneth: in the morning he shall devour the prey, and at night he shall divide the spoil.

Genesis 49:27

Benjamin
12

JESSE, THE FATHER OF DAVID. In Judah, Jesse is rooted and so, ultimately, is Jesus.

Benjamin was uprooted. Over and over throughout history the Jews have been uprooted, taken from one land, forced to live in another, in exile. By the waters of Babylon have they hung up their harps, strangers in a strange land.

Joseph's aloneness before the return of his brothers is almost as incomprehensible to us as it was to his servant.

We live in an uprooted society. For Hugh and me Crosswicks was a place to put down roots, to belong to a community, a community that was rooted in the white-spired church at the crossroads.

Joseph, despite his feelings of alienation, despite being a stranger in a strange land, had nevertheless put down roots in Egypt. He was rooted by his work, which he could not leave. He was rooted by Asenath and his sons, whom he would not leave. He did not consider going back to Canaan and his father's house, the place of his coat of many colours, and of his grand dreams which were now being fulfilled.

Instead, he begged his brothers to go back to Canaan for their father, Jacob, and to bring him back to Egypt. *"And you shall dwell in the land of Goshen, and you shall be near me, you and your children, and your herds, and all that you have, and then I will nourish you, for there are yet five years of famine, lest you, and all your household, and all that you have, come to poverty. And behold, your eyes see, and the eyes of my brother, Benjamin, that it is my mouth that speaks to you. And you shall tell my father of all my glory in Egypt, and shall haste and bring my father here."*

"All my glory in Egypt." Joseph wanted his father to know. How human was the great man!

And Joseph flung his arms around Benjamin's neck and wept again and then he kissed all of his brothers, until their eyes lost their terror and they were able to speak with him.

The land of Goshen. That was where Joseph asked Pharaoh to let him settle his father and his brothers. Crosswicks sits high on a ridge a mile from the village of Goshen in the Litchfield Hills. It is a land that was colonized in the very early eighteenth century by people deeply steeped in Scripture. Canaan is not far away from us, and Bethlehem not much further. But Goshen is our village, where the beautiful old colonial church stands with its white spire, the highest spire in the state, not because the spire is unusually tall, but because Goshen is the highest (and coldest, and windiest) spot in the state.

How different it is in every way from Goshen in Egypt, where Benjamin was to plant new roots. Even after two visits to Egypt I find it hard to visualize the land of Goshen in which Joseph settled his family, because our rolling green dairy farm hills are imprinted in my mind's eye.

Goshen, a land of welcome. In gratitude, Pharaoh opened wide his arms and invited all of Joseph's family to come to Egypt. Benjamin, who had lived in Canaan all his life, was journeying into the unknown. Hugh and I took our children and moved them from Goshen back to New York and the world of the theatre where we all had to put down new roots. New York is the place of my birth, and so it will always be home, but in leaving Goshen and returning to the great city we were moving into the unknown, not knowing what the future would hold. Of course we never know. Futures are roughly and irrevocably altered by unexpected accidents, betrayals, illnesses. What we have is this day, this moment.

Joseph moved his family to Egypt, to the land of Goshen, and there Benjamin and his brothers were able to put down new roots. But all earthly roots are only fibers, tender and temporary. Ultimately, another pharaoh down the line would be threatened by the prosperity of the Jews, and then would begin the great epic of Moses and the Exodus.

After Hugh's death once again I moved into the unknown. I stayed in Crosswicks until after Christmas, then moved back to New York and the scaffolded apartment and a new life with college students, and how blessed I was to have them there.

Then, at last, the scaffolding came down, and I had to think about redecorating the apartment, something which Hugh and I knew would have to be done as soon as the scaffolding was gone, and the rain stopped seeping into the living room ceiling. Why does everything take at least twice as long as it is expected to take? Charlotte and

I lived out of boxes and in chaos for well over a year. Redecorating was complicated by a leak in the washing machine in the apartment above us, a slow leak which declared itself by blowing out our kitchen lights. We had to wait for leprous looking walls to dry before we could do anything about the kitchen. But now it's done, and it is beautiful—or, at least, it's almost done. But it's finished enough to be comfortably livable, and for us to resume our multigenerational dinner parties. Perhaps the rooms, clean and light, do not look as they would if Hugh and I had done them together, but that's something that's no longer possible. It is perhaps more of a woman's apartment than it was, but then, Charlotte and I are women.

One night as I was getting ready for bed after a dinner party, during which many people had commented on how lovely the apartment was, I thought to myself, "I hate the apartment this way. I want it all back exactly the way it was." I knew this was irrational. I knew the apartment was lovely. And suddenly I realized that of course what I wanted was not the apartment back the way it was. I wanted Hugh back. Once I realized that, I was able to let it all go and take a good hot bath and get into bed and read and relax before going to sleep.

It is helpful that sometimes we can understand the real motives underlying some of our irrationality. I think Joseph always knew that he would not feel complete until he had been reconciled with his brothers.

As I continue to move out into the unknown the only thing I know is that I still believe with Paul that *all things work together for good to them that love God*—not just in this mortal life, but in God's ultimate purpose for Creation which we are called on to observe and contemplate. It may be that our contemplation will involve great pain.

And sometimes our pain will be deepened as we struggle to remember that its purpose is love.

I am grateful that I was able to honour my promise to Hugh all the way to the end, to be with him when he died. We had promised each other no death-prolonging machinery, and with all my heart I thank the doctors who allowed him to die when the time came for death, a good and holy death, a beginning of a new journey.

Paul goes on to ask, *Who shall separate us from the love of Christ? Shall tribulation, or distress, or persecution, or famine, or nakedness, or peril, or sword? . . . Nay, in all these things we are more than conquerors through him that loved us. For I am persuaded that neither death, nor life, nor angels, nor principalities, nor powers, nor things present, nor things to come, nor height, nor depth, nor any other creature, shall be able to separate us from the love of God which is in Christ Jesus our Lord.*

Powerful words. Words of high poetry and truth. Words to hold on to. Words which I have held to for many years.

When Paul speaks of angels and principalities and powers as trying to separate us from the love of God he is, of course, speaking of fallen angels, of the principalities and powers which have chosen to follow Satan rather than the Lord of Love. There are true angels, such as the three who came to Abraham; Gabriel, who appeared to young Mary; the angels who ministered to Jesus in the garden, and who have unfailingly followed their calling to be "ministering spirits." There are principalities and powers who eternally worship the Creator with hymns of joy. What God has created is good, and it is a part of the fallenness of all of Creation that some angels, as well as human beings, have turned in pride away from the

Creator. But the good angels are more powerful, the great principalities and powers are more loving, than all the fallenness and pride put together. We cannot be separated from the love of God.

> Ye watchers and ye holy ones,
> Bright seraphs, cherubim, and thrones,
> Raise the glad strain, Alleluia!
> Cry out, dominions, princedoms, powers,
> Virtues, archangels, angels' choirs,
> Alleluia, alleluia, alleluia, alleluia, alleluia!

Crosswicks is a place of roots for me, but it is also a place where I have known great pain, where I have clung to the strength of Paul's words. Four times in two years the phone rang to tell us of the death of close friends, deaths which would alter the patterns of our lives. Whenever the phone rings at an unusual hour my heart catapults back into the cold white grief of those phone calls. On the fourth evening of every month when I read the first lines of the 22nd psalm, *"My God, my God, why have you forsaken me?"* I am back in that strange room in the conference center the night after I learned of Hugh's cancer.

I remember a long-gone winter night when I sat waiting by the fire until two in the morning while a blizzard raged outside, and I waited for Hugh to come home. He had set out in the early afternoon on an errand of mercy, to drive a friend at a time of crisis a hundred miles north, into the teeth of the blizzard. I fed our children, put them to bed with the usual stories and songs and prayers, fed and walked the dogs, put the cats in the cellar for the night, kept feeding the fire. A little after two the dogs jumped up, tails wagging, and Hugh staggered in, exhausted, hungry, needing to be fed, loved. And our roots went even deeper into the land of Goshen.

But no place is safe, not even an isolated, dairy farm village. In the late fifties it seemed that war with Russia, nuclear war, was imminent. At school in the village the children were taught to crouch under their little wooden desks, their hands over their heads, in case an atom bomb fell on the school. As if that would protect them! What insanity! In the spring when the lilacs bloomed I wondered if there would be another spring, if Goshen would still be there, if we would ever smell the spring fragrance again, hear the peepers singing in the marsh.

Nothing can separate us from the love of God. Whatever happened, God would be with us, as God was with Shadrach, Meshach, and Abednego in the fiery furnace.

There are happier, more placid memories. Seeing my daughter Josephine kneeling beside the old wooden cradle in which her baby brother lay. (A snapshot of that is framed and on the wall.) Meals around the table, holding hands as we sang grace. Watching my mother walk down the lane, picking an assortment of weeds and wildflowers with which she always managed to create a beautiful arrangement.

The old house, like most old houses, is full of the richness of living, of joy and tears, birth and death, marrying and burying.

Five years ago Bion and Laurie moved in. Laurie had finished her hospital internship and residency. There is an excellent hospital in the nearby town which has attracted a group of fine physicians. Our son said, "Well, Mother and Dad, you taught us about multi-generational living."

And what a blessing it is to have them there. After Hugh's death there was no way I could have kept Crosswicks on my own. It would have had to be sold. And now it is Bion's and Laurie's home, and the pattern has changed as the pattern changed for Jacob when he moved with his sons from the land of Canaan to the land of Goshen. No mention is made of Dinah in this move. We do not know what happened to Dinah.

Jacob and his sons and their wives and their children and their flocks and their herds moved to the land of Goshen. But their roots, their hearts, were not in Egypt, but in the land from which they had come, from home. In his last days, Jacob asked to be taken home to be buried. And so, later on, did Joseph.

Years ago when my children were young, my mother did not want to come to us, to Crosswicks, for Christmas, and I did not understand. She loved us and the children. I was her only child, our three children were her only grandchildren. Why didn't she want to come?

After Hugh's death my daughters each urged me to come to them at Christmas. I love my daughters. I love my grandchildren. But I didn't want to go to them at Christmas. It was a strong, visceral feeling. I needed to be where my roots are. At last I understood my mother.

It was the famine that drove Jacob away from home and into the land of Goshen. He was an old man, and before he died in that foreign land he gathered his children about him. Jacob had not only his own twelve sons, but Joseph's two sons, Manasseh and Ephraim, who appear to have been favoured above the children of all the other sons, who are not even mentioned when Jacob dispenses his blessings.

When old Jacob saw Joseph's sons he asked who they were, and Joseph replied, *"They are my sons, whom God has given me here."*

Jacob was deeply moved, saying, *"I had not thought to see your face, and lo, God has let me see your children also."* And he called the boys to him to be blessed.

The blessing harks back a generation; just as Jacob replaced his elder brother, Esau, when Isaac blessed his sons, so Jacob gave primary blessing to Ephraim, the younger of the two boys, once again overturning the rule of primogeniture.

When Joseph saw his father placing his right hand on Ephraim's head he was displeased; so he took hold of his father's hand to move it from Ephraim's head to Manasseh's head. Joseph said to him, "No, my father, this one is the firstborn; put your right hand on his head."

And his father refused, and said, "I know, my son, I know. He also shall become a people, and he also shall be great; but truly his younger brother shall be greater than he, and his seed shall become a multitude of nations." And he blessed them that day, saying, "God made thee as Ephraim and Manasseh; and he made Ephraim before Manasseh." Joseph was not pleased with this, but a blessing given cannot be withdrawn.

Jacob spoke to each of his twelve sons, in order of their birth, but he did not make his first-born Reuben the foremost of the brothers. Reuben still had to pay for his night with Bilhah.

It was Judah who was the favoured son. *"The sceptre shall not depart from Judah,"* Jacob prophesied, *"nor the ruler's staff from between his feet."*

To Joseph he promised that God almighty would bless him *"with blessings of heaven above, blessings of the deep that couches beneath, blessings of the breasts, and of the womb. The blessings of your father are mighty beyond the blessings of the eternal mountains, the bounties of an everlasting life."*

And his blessing of Benjamin seems strange indeed, little Benjamin who seems to have caused no one any trouble. *"Benjamin is like a vicious wolf. Morning and evening he kills and devours."*

There seems little indication that he did so, though God skips over him, and over Joseph, to choose Judah as the brother from whose tribe the great king David would spring. Perhaps in a prophetic way Jacob was seeing his son's fierce descendants—the Benjamite warriors like Ehud and Saul and Jonathan—famed for their archery.

When Jacob yielded up the ghost and was gathered unto his people, Joseph fell upon his father's face, and wept upon him, and kissed him. And Joseph commanded the physicians who served him to embalm his father, and the physicians embalmed Israel. And forty days were fulfilled for him, for so are fulfilled the days of those who are embalmed, and the Egyptians mourned for him threescore and ten days.

Again that extraordinary number, forty!

But when the days of his mourning were past, Joseph spoke unto the house of Pharaoh, saying, "If now I have found grace in your eyes, speak, I pray you, in the ears of Pharaoh, saying, My father made me swear, saying, Lo, I die. In my grave which I have digged for me in the land of Canaan, there shalt thou bury me. Now therefore let me go up, I pray thee, and bury my father, and I will come again." And Pharaoh said, "Go up, and bury thy father, according as he made thee swear."

So Joseph went to bury his father.

And when Joseph's brothers saw that their father was dead, they said, "Perhaps Joseph will hate us, and will certainly require us all the evil which we did to him." Like many of us, they could not believe that they were forgiven for what they had done. Joseph had welcomed them into the land of Goshen, and treated them with love and kindness, once he had revealed himself to them as Joseph, and still they were afraid. *And they sent a messenger to Joseph, saying, So shall you say to Joseph, "Forgive, I beg you, forgive the trespasses the servants of your father's God have done."* And Joseph wept when he heard their words.

And his brothers fell down before his face, and they said, "Behold, we are your servants."

And Joseph said to them, "Do not be afraid, for am I in the place of God? But as for you, you thought evil against me, but God meant it for good, to bring to pass, as it happened, that many people have been saved alive from starvation. So do not fear: I will nourish you, and your little ones." And he comforted them, and spoke kindly to them.

All things worked together for good to Joseph, for he loved God. Terrible things happened to him, and wonderful things happened to him, and Joseph grew strong and compassionate, very different as a man from the spoiled bragging brat he had been as a child.

Indeed his brothers did bow down before him, but that was no longer what was important. What was important was that because Joseph had come to love God in this land of strangers, he no longer needed to brag, to thrust himself onto centre stage. He had learned to love.

I know that all things work together for good as God ultimately works out the creative and loving purpose of the universe. Just as Joseph learned to understand that

God could use the wickedness of his brothers—in selling him into Egypt—for the saving of many lives from the slow and agonizing death of starvation, so God can come into all that happens to us, our griefs and our joys, and use them for good towards the coming of the kingdom.

Simeon and Levi, who slaughtered Shechem and all his tribe, and all the brothers when they conspired to kill Joseph, and when they sold him into Egypt, were indeed a horror and a hissing and an everlasting reproach. But through the prophet Jeremiah God not only warns, he encourages, *"My people, do not be afraid, I will come to you and save you. I will make you well again; I will heal your wounds. People of Israel, I have always loved you, so I continue to show you my constant love. The time is coming when I will make a new covenant with the people of Israel. It will not be like the old covenant . . . The new covenant will be this: I will put my law within you and write it in your hearts."*

For God is indeed a God of mercy, waiting for us to say, "I'm sorry! I want to come home!" And then the Almighty arms are opened to receive us into joy.

Joseph's life, with its sudden reversals of fortune, was more dramatic than most of our lives. But I have learned much from him on my journey towards becoming human. Surely after his brothers sold him into Egypt he learned how to observe and contemplate, looking *out* on all that was around him, rather than *in* towards his own pride and arrogance. In Egypt he learned to see everything as belonging to God: his dreams; the stars at night; the prisoners under his care; Asenath, his wife, and their two sons; the starving people who, like the prisoners, were entrusted to his care, and for the appeasing of whose hunger he was responsible. He had learned to live in the moment, rather than in the projections of his grandiose dreams. It was only when he let his pride go that there was any possibility of the dreams being fulfilled.

We, too, are to live in the moment, the very now. Our roots are deep in the past, but our branches reach up into the future. In the present we observe and contemplate all that God has made, and all that we, with our stiff-necked pride and greed and judgmentalism, have made of what God has made. Are we not created to love and care for our planet, and to love each other enough to live in peace? If we love God, then the Source of Love can come into our lives with redemptive power.

This past Sunday when I knelt at the altar in church, the minister put the bread into my hands, and I took it into my mouth. That morsel of bread, my hands, the minister's hands on my head as he prayed for me, all the other people in church, in other churches, on the streets, alone, all, all, are made of the same stuff as the stars, that original stuff with which Jesus clothed himself when he came to live with us. I ate the bread, took the cup, and with it all the truth of the stories that tell us about ourselves as human beings. And I was as close to Joseph as I was to the people on either side of me.

After church I went home for lunch with a few of the people who had shared communion with me. I had made a mess of pottage, that mixture of lentils, onions, and rice, which Joseph's father, Jacob, sold to Esau for his birthright. It wasn't nice of Jacob to sell it and defraud his brother, but the pottage was a tempting dish. Friends, food, the love of God, all calling us to be human—not infallible, but human.

We are amazing, we human beings. We do wonderful things, and we do terrible things—but, above all, we make marvellous stories.

* * *

Joseph

Sometimes at night, after Asenath and our boys are asleep, I go to the temple to speak to my father-in-law, the high priest of On. The temple is made of stones that gleam with the gold of the sun god he serves. The stones are fitted together so that not even the thinnest blade of knife or sword can slip between them. On the day when night and day are the same length, neither one shorter or longer than the other, the midday sun moves through the portals and strikes all the way through the chambers of the temple to touch the altar.

One night, because he knows that numbers are beautiful to me, he worked them out for me, the movement of the heavenly bodies and the days and nights and months, so that I understood the calculations, and how the temple had been built, just so, so that he could know the very moment when the rays of the sun would reach the altar. A holiest of holy days. He knows, he says; he can do the purest mathematics, he says, because the sun does not move around the earth, he says. Instead, the earth moves around the sun, and the moon around the earth. His beautiful numbers are very persuasive. Would it disturb the Maker of the Universe if this were so?

At night he takes me out and shows me stars that are not just pricks of light, he says, but heavenly bodies like our earth, that dance around the sun. It is a holy dance, he says, this circling of the sun who is his god.

How strange it seems to me. I can see that the heavenly bodies which he tells me are not stars are different from the stars—steadier, less sparkling. We watch the great night sky, and he asks me about my God. I tell him of my great-grandfather, Abraham, who was taken out into the desert at night.

"Count the stars if you can," my God told Abraham. "So shall your descendants be."

"And has it happened?" asked the priest of On.

"It is happening," I tell him rashly, and I think of my brothers at home, so far away, and I wonder about their wives and their children. What is happening at home I do not know, nor if my father is still alive, nor my little brother, Benjamin. And yet I know that God's promises are never empty, and that it is through God's promise that I have been brought to this alien land and given power far beyond anything I could have had at home. Power beyond my dreams.

My father-in-law, the priest of On, says, "Then if your great-grandfather's descendants are to be as many as the stars in the sky, there will be jealousy of them."

He may be right. I know all about jealousy.

Sometimes we talk about our dreams. I had a dream in which I watched my father bless the Pharaoh, and I and my father were together once again. Will that happen? My father blessing the Pharaoh? And I and my father together once again? It was a dream of comfort.

The priest of On nods, but sadly, for, he says, he will die before that time of fulfillment. He is old, old and wise. He tells me of his dreams. He dreams of strange chariots, bearing people, flying across the sky. He dreams of buildings towering higher than the highest temples. He dreams of a great cloud that is brighter than a million suns. These dreams, he says, may or may not come to pass, depending on the paths chosen. He tells me of his dreams, but they are in a strange language which does not lend itself to interpretation. And though God does not give me the interpretation, I sense that these dreams are not against the plan of God. And I am troubled.

He laughs and tells me that he has dreamed of a child of God who will come to save us. "But I will be long dead before he comes," he tells me, "and you, too, and your children, and your children's children."

He questions me about my life at home, and about my brothers, and about the journey to Egypt. He wags his head as I tell him about Potiphar's wife, and I cannot tell what he thinks. He asks me about my time in prison, and I tell him of a foreign sailor who came there with a ring in his nose. He had been captain of a ship and he talked of the four corners of the earth, and how his sailors had feared they would sail off the edge, where strange and fearful monsters waited, and they had rebelled and cast him out of his ship, and a sea god found him a log which carried him to shore. And the priest of On laughed deep in his throat and talked once more about the great dancing circles of the earth and stars.

I listen to many stories of gods who live in the sun, and in the sea, and in the moon, and also in strange beasts. I do not know whether my father-in-law, the priest of On, believes in these gods, or only in the sun.

His eyes are bright as he talks about the sun god who holds the heavenly bodies that dance around it, but never come close. For them, to come close would be to burn. The sun god is fire, and fire burns, and does not care about what is burned.

The God who showed my great-grandfather Abraham the stars walks with us. That is the difference. The sun god shines with brilliance but does not touch its people. The God of my fathers, of Abraham, Isaac, and Jacob, is with us. When my brothers threw me into the pit,

God was there, in the pit with me. When I ruled over Potiphar's household, God was there in my ruling. When I refused Potiphar's wife because I would not dishonour my master, God was there in my refusing. When I was in prison, God was there in my bondage. In my days of power, God is with me, guiding me.

And is God with my brothers and my father? When Simeon and Levi killed Shechem, did they escape God? Or when my brothers sold me into Egypt was not God there? with them? with me?

If my heart is cold towards my brothers, does not that also chill the heart of God?

The sun god looks down but is not part of the lives of those who worship the burning light. But my God—how can we bear a God who cares?

The high priest of On can turn away from those who disobey him or those who hurt him or those he does not love. He can condemn them to death.

Oh, my brothers, because God is with us, how can I turn away from you without turning away from God?

Oh, yes, my father-in-law, you who are the high priest of On, the sun burns, but it burns not because it is a god but because it was made by God, to burn me until I love my brothers once again.

Oh, my brothers, I thank you for all that you gave me when you sold me into Egypt. Because of you, it is my riches of understanding that I value, not my palace and my power. Yes, the sun burns, burns away anger and outrage, and my heart opens like a lotus flower.

And now my brothers have come, oh my brothers, and now that I love them, and they are freed to love me, joy will come again, and laughter.

And I will praise God.